CAMBRIDGE for ESOL

PHOTOCOPIABLE

ESOL Activities

UNIVERSITY PRESS

CAMBRIDGE UNIVERSITY PRESS
Cambridge, New York, Melbourne, Madrid, Cape Town, Singapore, São Paulo, Delhi

Cambridge University Press
The Edinburgh Building, Cambridge CB2 8RU, UK

www.cambridge.org
Information on this title: www.cambridge.org/9780521712385
© Cambridge University Press 2008

It is normally necessary for written permission for copying to be
obtained *in advance* from a publisher. The worksheets and the audioscript
at the back of this book are designed to be copied and distributed in class.
The normal requirements are waived here and it is not necessary to write
to Cambridge University Press for permission for an individual teacher to
make copies for use within his or her own classroom. Only those pages
which carry the wording '© Cambridge University Press' may be copied.

First published 2008

Printed in the United Kingdom at the University Press, Cambridge

A catalogue record for this publication is available from the British Library

ISBN 978-0-521-712385

Cambridge University Press has no responsibility for the persistence or
accuracy of URLs for external or third-party internet websites referred to in
this publication, and does not guarantee that any content on such websites is,
or will remain, accurate or appropriate. Whilst factual information given in
this work is correct at the time of going to print, Cambridge University Press
does not guarantee the accuracy of such information thereafter.

Contents

Map of the book

Theme	Unit	Type of activity	Function summary	Grammar summary	AECC*	Skills for Life †
1 At college	1a How do you spell that?	introducing yourself	asking for and spelling names	*to be* first and third person	Lr/E1.2e, Lr/E1.4b, Rw/E1.3a	Unit 1
	1b Timetables	reading a basic college timetable	talking about days and times	*to be* third person; *yes/no* questions; *where/what* questions	Rw/E1.3b, Sc/E1.1a, Ww/E1.1a	Unit 1
	1c Personal details	writing a short note about someone	asking for personal details	*to be* third person; *Wh-* questions	Ww/E1.1a, Wt/E1.1	Unit 1
2 All about me	2a Where are you from?	completing a table	talking about yourself	*to be* second and third persons; *Wh-* questions	Sc/E1.3a, Sc/E1.4b, Lr/E1.2e	Unit 1
	2b I live in a flat	reading maps and texts	talking about where you live	present simple regular verbs – *live*; prepositions *in, near, next to, on*	Rs/E1.1b, Sc/E1.1b, Sc/E1.3a	Unit 1
	2c New home	writing addresses; writing about where you live	describing people and places	*we've got …*	Wt/E1.1	Unit 1
3 In class	3a Can you say that again?	classroom language	asking for repetition, spelling and clarification	affirmative imperatives	Sc/E1.3d, Lr/E1.1d, Lr/E1.5b	Unit 1
	3b Class rules	reading college rules	talking about rules	negative imperatives	Rs/E1.1a, Rt/E1.2	Unit 1
	3c A note to college	writing a letter to college; writing greetings and endings	apologising	*would like; is it possible to …?*	Ws/E1.2, Ws/E1.3	Unit 1
4 Times and schedules	4a Time	telling the time	asking for and giving times	*wh-* questions	Sc/E1.4a, Lr/E1.2c, Lr/E1.4b	Unit 2
	4b College trip	reading a poster for a college trip	saying months	present simple questions with third person plural; prepositions *at/in*	Rs/E1.1a, Rt/E1.1b, Sc/E1.4a	Unit 2
	4c A visit	writing a letter to join a college trip	saying dates	*would like*	Ws/E1.1	Unit 2
5 Family life	5a Morning	speaking about your day	talking about routines	present simple first person; *yes/no* questions; short answers	Sc/E1.4a, Lr/E1.2c, Lr/E1.4b	Unit 2
	5b My family	reading a family tree and completing a text	talking about your family	*have got*; possessives	Rs/E1.1a, Rt/E1.1a, Sc/E1.3b	Unit 8
	5c Julia's day	writing about your partner's day	asking for information	present simple third person; spelling of third person endings	Ws/E1.3, Ww/E1.1c	Unit 2
6 Shopping	6a At the market	buying food and saying prices	making requests	questions with *How much …?*; countable nouns	Sc/E1.2a, Le/E1.1c, Lr/E1.2e	Unit 3
	6b Going shopping	reading an information leaflet	asking for information	*Wh-* questions	Rt/E1.1b, Rw/E1.3b, Sc/E1.3b	Unit 3
	6c A shopping list	writing a shopping list	writing reminders	containers and determiners of quantity; *remember to, don't forget to*	Ww/E1.1c	Unit 3

* AECC = Adult ESOL Core Curriculum † Skills for Life = *Skills for Life Learner Materials E1* published by the Department for Education and Skills

Map of the book

Theme	Unit	Type of activity	Function summary	Grammar summary	AECC*	Skills for Life †
7 Home	7a Welcome	welcoming someone to your home and showing them around	greeting and offering	prepositions of place; *What a (nice) ... !*	Sd/E1.1a, Lr/E1.1a, Lr/E1.2b	Unit 7
	7b A flat to rent	reading a description of a place to rent	describing your room	*next to, under, to the left/right of, in the middle of, opposite*	Rt/E1.1b, Sc/E1.4a, Lr/E1.2e	Unit 7
	7c My room	writing a description of a room	describing your room	*next to, under, on the left/right of, on the back of, opposite*	Wt/E1.1, Ws/E1.1, Lr/E1.2a	Unit 7
8 Sports, hobbies and interests	8a Sports, hobbies and interests	completing a table about hobbies	talking about ability	*can/can't*	Sc/E1.4a, Lr/E1.2b, Lr/E1.2e	
	8b Sports rules	reading about sports rules	regulations and rules	*can/can't*; location: *in front of, behind, in the middle of*	Rt/E1.1a, Sc/E1.4a, Sc/E1.4d	
	8c Our sports centre	filling in an application form for a sports centre	talking about ability	*good at, interested in, quite/very well*	Wt/E1.1, Ws/E1.1	
9 Transport	9a A single to Oxford Street	buying a ticket	making requests	present continuous affirmative	Sc/E1.2a, Sc/E1.3b, Lr/E1.2e	Unit 4
	9b Travel pass	reading a brochure	asking for information	*any + thing/where/ time/one*	Rt/E1.1b, Rt/E1.2, Sc/E1.4a	Unit 4
	9c Travelling	writing about preferences	expressing likes and preferences	*like + -ing* form	Ws/E1.1, Wt/E1.1	Unit 4
10 Directions	10a Can you tell me the way to the bus station?	drawing routes; completing directions	asking for directions	prepositions of direction	Sc/E1.3b, Sc/E1.3c, Lr/E1.3b	Unit 6
	10b Visitors' day	reading directions to a college open day	saying how far somewhere is	*How long does it take ... ?, How far ... ?, How many kilometres ... ?*	Rs/E1.1a, Rt/E1.1b	Unit 6
	10c Where's the party?	writing directions	giving directions	*until* for distances	Wt/E1.1, Ws/E1.1	Unit 6
11 Jobs	11a What's my job?	a quiz about jobs	asking for information	present simple *yes/no* questions and short answers	Sc/E1.4d, Lr/E1.1c, Lr/E1.4b	Unit 10
	11b Person wanted	reading job advertisements	understanding abbreviations	*needed, wanted*	Rs/E1.1a, Rt/E1.1b	Unit 10
	11c A job application	writing a simple letter for a job	describing your character	*would like*	Wt/E1.1, Ws/E1.3, Sc/E1.1b	Unit 10
12 Food	12a Would you like a drink?	offering food and drink	making offers and requests; talking about likes and dislikes	*Would you like ...?, Could I ...?, Can I ...?*	Sc/E1.4d, Lr/E1.2e, Sd/E1.1c	
	12b A menu	reading a menu	understanding menus		Rs/E1.1a, Rt/E1.1b, Rt/E1.2	
	12c A recipe	writing a recipe	giving instructions	imperatives; countable and uncountable nouns; linking with *when*	Ws/E1.1, Ws/E1.2	

* AECC = Adult ESOL Core Curriculum † Skills for Life = *Skills for Life Learner Materials E1* published by the Department for Education and Skills

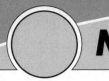

Map of the book

Theme	Unit	Type of activity	Function summary	Grammar summary	AECC*	Skills for Life †
13 Clothes and weather	13a The weather	practising a conversation	talking about the weather	present continuous affirmative	Sc/E1.4a, Sc/E1.4d, Lr/E1.2e	Unit 8
	13b Great British weather	reading an article about weather in Britain	talking about the weather	*generally, around, about*	Rs/E1.1a, Rt/E1.1a	Unit 8
	13c Clothes	writing a description of what you are wearing	describing clothes	basic order of adjectives (age, colour, material)	Wt/E1.1, Ws/E1.1	Unit 9
14 Health	14a At the doctor's	listening to a conversation at a doctor's	making an appointment; describing symptoms	*have got*	Sd/E1.1b, Lr/E1.2c, Lr/E1.3a	Unit 5
	14b Medicine labels	reading medicine labels	understanding instructions	*How much ...? / How many ...?*	Rs/E1.1a, Rt/E1.1b	Unit 5
	14c An absence note	writing a note of absence	saying sorry; wishing someone well	present continuous affirmative and negative	Ws/E1.1, Ws/E1.3	Unit 5
15 At the Post Office	15a Sending a parcel	transactions in a post office	making requests	*Can I ... / Can you ...?; Could you...?; Have you got ... ?*	Sc/E1.2a, Sd/E1.1b, Lr/E1.5c	
	15b Special delivery	reading instructions about how to complete a special delivery form	understanding instructions	sequencing words: *then, next, first*	Rw/E1.1, Rw/E1.3b, Rt/E1.1b	
	15c Thank you	writing a note to thank someone	phrases for giving and receiving presents	*What a (great) ... !*	Ww/E1.1a, Ws/E1.1	
16 Social language	16a After you	practising everyday social language	polite social expressions		Sd/E1.1a, Lr/E1.4a, Lr/E1.5a	
	16b Good manners	reading a quiz about customs and manners	talking about customs and manners	*when* + subject + verb	Rs/E1.1a, Rt/E1.1b	
	16c A card for you	writing cards for different occasions	expressions for different social occasions		Rw/E1.2, Wt/E1.1, Ww/E1.1a	

* AECC = Adult ESOL Core Curriculum   † Skills for Life = *Skills for Life Learner Materials E1* published by the Department for Education and Skills

Thanks and acknowledgements

Author's thanks

The author would like to thank his students and colleagues for teaching him about ESOL. The author would also like to thank Nóirín Burke, Hazel Meek, Brigit Viney and Anna Gunn for their help in writing *ESOL Activities Entry 1*.

This one is for Joe.

Publisher's acknowledgements

The author and publishers would like to thank all the ESOL professionals who reviewed the material: Kathryn Alevizos, Penelope Campbell, Margot Farnham and Ruth Taylor.

The authors and publishers acknowledge the following sources of copyright material and are grateful for the permissions granted. While every effort has been made, it has not always been possible to identify the sources of all the material used, or to trace all copyright holders. If any omissions are brought to our notice, we will be happy to include the appropriate acknowledgements on reprinting.

p. 43 and p. 111: The Trafford Centre for the simplified Trafford Centre Floor Map. Copyright © the Trafford Centre Limited; p. 97: Royal Mail Group for the simplified text 'Royal Mail Special Delivery'. Special Delivery™ is a Trade Mark of Royal Mail Group Ltd. Reproduced by kind permission of Royal Mail Group Ltd. All Rights Reserved.

Photo on p. 31 (top): Alamy/Mediacolor's; on p.31 (bottom): Alamy/PCL; p. 67: David Haggerton.

Proofreading by Sarah Hall.
Recordings produced by Ian Harker, edited by Benje Noble, recorded at The Soundhouse Ltd, London.
Illustrations by Kathryn Baker, Julian Mosedale and Kamae Design.

Introduction

Who is *ESOL Activities Entry 1* for?

ESOL Activities Entry 1 is for teachers of ESOL in colleges and schools in the UK. It contains photocopiable material for classroom work and can be used to supplement other ESOL material, such as the *Skills for Life Learner Materials E1* published by the Department for Education and Skills (DFES). The activities provide self-contained lessons for the busy teacher as well as ready-made homework or self-study exercises. They are aimed at the mid-range Entry 1 learner attending a course at that level. These are learners who would be expected to move to the following level after completion of the course, usually after one year.

How is *ESOL Activities Entry 1* organised?

There are 16 general themes connected with life in the UK. Each of these contains three units based on the sub-themes of Speaking and listening, Reading, and Writing. The units are all linked to the Adult ESOL Core Curriculum (AECC) and can be used to supplement existing material, offering diversity and a refreshing approach to these useful and familiar themes. The Map of the book provides a clear overview of the 48 units, including references to the AECC and the *Skills for Life Learner Materials E1* for each unit. This enables the teacher to quickly locate a suitable unit for their class.

How is each unit organised?

Each unit consists of two pages. The left-hand page has step-by-step Teacher's notes explaining the procedure for each unit as well as other useful information such as the relevant AECC reference and answers to the exercises. The right-hand page is a photocopiable worksheet. Each worksheet is designed to take approximately 30 minutes, and they all require minimal preparation. The Teacher's notes include a key information panel with the following headings:

Type of activity: an explanation of what the unit will involve
AECC reference: AECC descriptors appropriate for the level and the focus of the unit
Aim(s): the aims for learners
Language: a description of the functions and grammar targeted in the unit
Vocabulary: a list of vocabulary which needs pre-teaching, plus any key vocabulary in the unit
Preparation: notes on how to prepare prior to the lesson, e.g. photocopying or cutting up activity cards
Differentiation: activities which can be used as an option with weaker or stronger learners.

Each unit is divided into three stages – a *warmer* to get the learners thinking about the topic of the unit, the *main activities*, and an *extension* activity in order to help learners to apply their learning outside the classroom. Each unit practises a main skill although other skills are integrated into each sheet. Each unit also has *self-study exercises* which learners can do for homework to consolidate classroom learning. These exercises are at the back of the book. Some of these are intended to extend learners' familiarity with vocabulary, structures or functions utilised in the worksheet. Other exercises are simple revision to reinforce learning and act as a reminder of what has been covered by the worksheet.

How will *ESOL Activities Entry 1* help my students?

Warmer: These activites are designed as a light introduction to the lesson to get learners thinking about the topic of the lesson. As an alternative warmer, teachers may find it more appropriate to simply discuss what learners know about the topic, e.g. the functions and services of the Post Office.

Speaking and listening: These activities focus on interactions that learners may encounter in everyday life. The speaking activities give learners an opportunity to practise functional language in situations they will encounter, such as at the market or at the doctor's, as well as practising appropriate responses and helping their pronunciation. The listening activities practise strategies to help learners' general understanding and how to manage basic social interactions.

Reading: The texts in *ESOL Activities Entry 1* are mainly based on authentic material that learners may come across in their everyday lives. The activities enable learners to develop and practise strategies for understanding a range of texts that they may be required to read outside the classroom. Generally the activities are designed to help learners of this level understand simple texts.

Writing: These activities are designed to highlight the key elements of writing that will help learners deal with this skill in everyday life and in any ESOL exams they may wish to take. They focus on basic features of writing that learners may be faced with at this level, for example spelling, form-filling, notes and simple letters.

What is the best way to use *ESOL Activities Entry 1* in the classroom?

The worksheets are designed to be photocopied, taken into class and used as a set of activities. Teachers can choose the most appropriate worksheet for the language they are practising at the time. For example, units 9a, b and c (Transport) tie in with unit 4 (Local transport) in the *Skills for Life Learner Materials E1*. The reference to these materials in the Map of the book should help teachers decide on the most appropriate unit for their purposes. The activities can also be exploited beyond what is given in the Teacher's notes. Teachers may wish to develop the material in the following ways:

Speaking
- Ask learners to remember short conversations presented in the worksheets and role-play them.
- Adapt conversations presented in the worksheets to reflect local references and circumstances.
- Where possible, try to practise the pronunciation of the key words in all the worksheets.

Listening
- Copy the audioscript with key words blanked out and ask learners to fill them in as they listen again.
- Use the recordings for dictation where the recording is not too long.
- Copy the audioscript, cut it up and ask learners to put the pieces in order as they listen again.

Reading
- Use the reading texts to practise and develop all the vocabulary from them. You can copy the text with key vocabulary blanked out for learners to fill in, either in class or for homework.
- Use the texts for revision at a later date, by asking learners what they remember about a certain topic, and then giving them the text again to consolidate their learning and increase their confidence.
- Read the texts to the learners to consolidate the sound–spelling links.

Writing
- Copy the model text with key vocabulary blanked out for learners to fill in.
- Copy the model text, cut it up and ask learners to put the pieces in the correct order.
- Copy learner-produced texts onto OHTs (with learners' names blanked out) for learners to correct spelling and grammar errors.

ESOL Activities is also available at Entry 2 and Entry 3.

1a How do you spell that?

Type of activity
Spelling common names. Class and pair work.

AECC reference
Lr/E1.2e, Lr/E1.4b, Rw/E1.3a

Aims
To give learners practice in listening to and asking for names and spelling them; they will practise the alphabet.

Language
asking for and spelling names; *to be* first and third persons; *How do you spell … ?*; *What's your name?*

Vocabulary
say, tea, cry, go, bed, car, spell, sorry

Preparation
Photocopy the worksheet. Optional: photocopy the alphabet table from exercise 4 and enlarge it to poster size.

Differentiation
Weaker learners: write the letters of the alphabet on the board and ask them to find and copy the vowels.
Stronger learners: teach *first name, middle name* and *surname* and ask them to change the conversation in exercise 7 so that they ask for this information too.

Warmer

Write letters A–Z on board and then write *Ahmed, Boris* next to A and B. Put learners into small groups and ask them to think of a name that begins with each letter of the alphabet. Set a time limit of two to three minutes and check answers with whole class.

1 Learners complete the list of vowels with lower and upper case letters. Practise the vowels.

Answers
a A   e E   i I   o O   u U

2 (▶2) Introduce yourself to one of your learners: 'Hello, I'm [Carmen]. [C-A-R-M-E-N].' Learners introduce themselves to their neighbour. Ask learners to listen and complete the names.

Answers
Jessica, David, Butri, Megan, Thomas, Zakir

3 Ask the learners to say the words.

4 Say letter *a* and get learners to tell you which word from the table it sounds like. Ask learners to complete the table with the remaining letters of the alphabet.

Answers
/ei/   a, h, j, k
/iː/   b, c, d, e, g, p, t, v
/aɪ/   i, y
/əʊ/   o
/uː/   q, u, w
/e/   f, l, m, n, s, x, z
/aː/   r

5 (▶3) Play the recording and ask the learners to say the names of the letters.

6 (▶4) Tell learners to read the sentences and then listen and complete the missing letters. Point out that we say *double–t* in *Charlotte* and that *ph* in the name *Joseph* is pronounced /f/.

Answers
1 Ahmed   2 Charlotte   3 Joseph

7 (▶5) Ask learners to read the short conversations and try to guess the missing words. Learners then listen and complete the conversations.

Answers
1 I'm   2 name's   3 you   4 spell

8 Put the learners into pairs and ask them to change the conversations in exercise 7 to use their own names, and practise.

Extension

Ask learners to go round the class and ask each other to spell their names. Learners write the names of all the learners in the class.

Answers: Self-study exercises   **How do you spell that?**   **Your own notes**

1 2 How do you spell Jack?
   3 How do you spell that?

2 C D E F G H I J K L M N O P Q R S T U V W X Y Z

3 2 is   3 how   4 spell   5 S-S-E-I-N

How do you spell that? 1a

1 Complete.

a / A   ..../..........   ..../..........   o / O   ..../..........

2 Listen and complete the names.

Jess..*i*..ca
D......vid
B......ri
M.....gan
Th......mas
Zak......r

3 Say the words.

say tea cry go you bed car

4 Complete the table with the letters.

a	b̶	c	d	e	f̶	g	h	i̶	j	k	l	m
n	o	p	q̶	r	s	t	u	v	w	x	y	z

say	tea	cry	go	you	bed	car
a	b	i		q	f	

5 Listen and practise.

6 Listen and complete.

1 I'm A.................... .   2 My name's C.................... .   3 Hello, I'm called J.................... .

7 Listen and complete.

1 David: What's your name?
  Butri: (1) .... Butri. That's B-U-T-R-I.

2 Thomas: Hello, my (2) .... Thomas.
  Butri: Sorry. How do (3) .... spell Thomas?
  Thomas: T-H-O-M-A-S.

3 Zakir: I'm Zakir.
  Megan: Sorry. How do you (4) .... that?
  Zakir: Z-A-K-I-R.

8 Work together. Choose a conversation from exercise 7 and practise, using your own names.

1b Timetables

Type of activity
Reading a timetable. Individual and pair work.

AECC reference
Rw/E1.3b, Sc/E1.1a, Ww/E1.1a

Aims
To give learners practice in saying subjects, days of the week and simple times.

Language
talking about days and times; *to be* third person; *yes/no* questions; *where/what* questions

Vocabulary
days; numbers 1–9; grammar, IT, listening, maths, reading, speaking, writing

Preparation
Photocopy the worksheet.

Differentiation
Weaker learners: ask them to cover the days and to try to write them again with correct spelling.
Stronger learners: teach them *morning, afternoon, evening, night*. Also teach them *weekend* and ask them which days are the weekend.

Warmer

Ask learners the days of the week. Ask them which days they come to college and which days they have a rest.

1 Revise the alphabet and tell them to complete the calendar.

> **Answers**
> 1 Monday   2 Tuesday   3 Wednesday   4 Thursday
> 5 Friday   6 Saturday   7 Sunday

2 (▶6) Play the recording. Learners listen and repeat the days of the week.

3 Ask learners to match the words with the pictures. Practise the pronunciation of the words.

> **Answers**
> 1 reading   2 writing   3 speaking   4 listening
> 5 grammar   6 maths   7 IT

4 Ask learners to read the timetable and answer the questions. Check learners understand the exercise by asking the whole class questions like *When does Zakir have a grammar lesson?*

> **Answers**
> 1 No   2 No   3 Yes   4 Yes   5 Yes
> 6 general English   7 room A1   8 speaking
> 9 room B8   10 IT

5 Ask learners to complete the blank timetable with subjects and rooms.

6 Revise and practise the questions *What's on … ?*, *Where's … ?* Then ask them to work in pairs and ask and answer questions to complete their second blank timetable with their partner's timetable. They write their partner's name above it.

Extension

Ask learners to talk to a friend about the subjects they study at college. Ask them to bring the list to next lesson and share it with the class.

Answers: Self-study exercises   **Timetables**   **Your own notes**

1 2 Tuesday   3 Wednesday   4 Thursday   5 Friday
6 Saturday   7 Sunday

2 2 Is listening on Monday morning?
3 Where's speaking on Wednesday?
4 What's on Wednesday morning?

Timetables 1b

1 Complete the calendar.

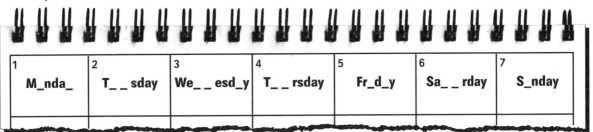

1	2	3	4	5	6	7
M_nda_	T_ _ sday	We_ _ esd_y	T_ _ rsday	Fr_d_y	Sa_ _ rday	S_nday

2 Listen and practise.

3 Label the pictures.

grammar   IT   listening   maths   reading   speaking   writing

1 ....   2 ....   3 ....   4 ....   5 ....   6 ....   7 ....

4 Read the timetable and answer the questions.

1 Is general English on Tuesday afternoon?
2 Is listening in classroom C1?
3 Is speaking on Wednesday afternoon?
4 Is IT in room A1?
5 Is maths on Friday morning?
6 What's on Monday morning?
7 Where's grammar on Wednesday?
8 What's on Wednesday afternoon?
9 Where's general English on Tuesday?
10 What's on Friday afternoon?

Timetable for Zakir Hussein – ESOL Entry 1
Teacher – Carmen Vernon

	Monday	Tuesday	Wednesday	Thursday	Friday
morning	general English	general English	grammar	general English	maths
room	A3	B8	A1	C3	B8
afternoon	listening	reading	speaking	writing	IT
room	C7	C3	C7	B8	A1

5 Write another timetable.

6 Work together. Ask questions to complete your partner's timetable.

A: What's on Monday morning?
B: On Monday morning it's general English.
A: Where is it?
B: It's in room B4.

My timetable

	Monday	Tuesday	Wednesday	Thursday	Friday
morning	general English				
room	B4				
afternoon					
room					

...............'s timetable

	Monday	Tuesday	Wednesday	Thursday	Friday
morning					
room					
afternoon					
room					

1c Personal details

Type of activity
Writing names, ages and numbers. Completing a form with basic personal details.

AECC reference
Ww/E1.1a, Wt/E1.1

Aims
To give learners practice in completing a simple form; practise asking about names and ages and revise saying numbers and letters.

Language
asking for personal details; *to be* third person; *Wh-* questions

Vocabulary
first name, surname, family name

Preparation
Make two sets of photocopies so that you have enough for one for each learner and enough to give one 'card' in exercise 3 to each learner.

Differentiation
Weaker learners: dictate some words from the unit, such as *address, surname, student* and *number*, and ask them to write them down.

Stronger learners: write details on the board about another fictional person and have them write about them. Alternatively, you could ask them to write about the Prime Minister: 10 Downing Street, London, SW1 2AA, UK or the Queen: Buckingham Palace, London, SW1A 1AA, UK.

Warmer

Ask learners if anyone has a student card and ask them what information is on it. Elicit *name, age, address, city, student number*.

1 Tell learners to complete the student card with the information from the box.

> **Answers**
> 1 Alamry   2 23   3 Birmingham   4 BM13

2 Ask learners to match the questions with the information from exercise 1.

> **Answers**
> 1 What's your surname?
> 2 How old are you?
> 3 Where do you live?
> 4 What's your student number?

3 Learners work in groups of four. Give each learner a role-card from exercise 3. Ask learners to read the information from their card and complete the table. Then tell learners to ask the other three people in their group and complete the rest of the table. Ask learners to cover up the cards on their worksheets so they can't see them while they do the exercise.

> **Answers**
>
> | First name | Surname | Age | City / Town | Student number |
> |---|---|---|---|---|
> | Isabel | Toth | 17 | Bradford | BC1A |
> | Muhammad | Shamsi | 33 | Dewsbury | BC10Q |
> | Hu | Yong | 24 | Leeds | BC8T |
> | Rahim | Yener | 49 | Shipley | BC4J |

4 Ask learners to look at their completed table and complete the text about Isabel.

> **Answers**
> 1 is   2 live   3 old   4 student number

5 Ask learners to use the text in exercise 4 to tell the class about themselves.

6 Ask learners to complete the table for the other learners. Model the conversation with a learner: *What's your first name/surname? How old are you? Where do you live? What's your student number?*

7 Ask stronger learners to write one or two sentences about another learner. Remind them to begin: *His/Her name is …*

Extension

Ask learners to write about a member of their family, a friend or someone they know.

Personal details

1 2 What's your name?
3 Where do you live?
4 What's your student number?

2 b 3   c 4   d 2

3 His name is Alex West. He is 45 years old. He lives in Leeds. His student number is UB 63.

Personal details 1c

1 Complete the student card.

| BM13 | Birmingham | Alamry | 23 |

City College Student Card

First name: Zakir
Surname (1) ....
Other names: Ali
Age: (2) ....
City/Town: (3) ....
Course: English (ESOL)
Student number: (4) ....

2 Match the questions with 1–4 in exercise 1.

How old are you? What's your surname? What's your student number? Where do you live?

3 Work in groups of four. Ask questions and complete the table.

First name	Surname	Age	City/Town	Student number
Isabel				
Muhammad				
Hu				
Rahim				

Name: Isabel Toth	Name: Muhammad Shamsi
Age: 17	Age: 33
City: Bradford	City: Dewsbury
Course: English (ESOL)	Course: English (ESOL)
Student number: BC1A	Student number: BC10Q
Name: Hu Yong	Name: Rahim Yener
Age: 24	Age: 49
City: Leeds	City: Shipley
Course: English (ESOL)	Course: English (ESOL)
Student number: BC8T	Student number: BC4J

4 Complete the text for Isabel.

My name (1) .... Isabel Toth. I (2) ....
in Bradford. I am 17 years (3) .... , and my
(4) .... is BC1A.

5 Tell the class about yourself.

6 Go round the class and get the same information from four learners.

First name	Surname	Age	City/Town	Student number

7 Write about another learner.

Dear …
I made a new friend at college today. His/Her name is …
He/She lives …

2a Where are you from?

Type of activity

Learners label maps of countries, listen to a quiz and walk round asking each other questions to complete a table. Class and pair work.

AECC reference

Sc/E1.3a, Sc/E1.4b, Lr/E1.2e

Aims

Learners will learn to say countries and nationalities, and talk about where they are from.

Language

talking about yourself; *to be* second and third persons; *Where are you from … ?*; *What language(s) do you speak?*

Vocabulary

countries, nationalities, languages

Preparation

Photocopy the worksheet. Take a world map to class.

Differentiation

Weaker learners: write up *Holland, England, China, Turkey* [stress pattern 1]; *Peru, Japan, Brazil* [stress pattern 2] on the board and ask them to group them according to the stress patterns in exercise 2. Stronger learners: ask them to write one or two sentences about the information in exercise 6: *Hasan is from Sudan. His nationality is Sudanese. He speaks Arabic and German.*

Warmer

Put learners into groups and give them three minutes to make a list of as many country names as they can. The group with the most names is the winner. If you have a world map, you could use it to elicit the names of more countries.

1 Ask learners to match the pictures with the country names.

> **Answers**
> 1 Scotland 2 Ireland 3 Iran 4 Iraq 5 Sudan
> 6 Poland

2 Tell learners to put the countries into groups according to the word stress.

> **Answers**
> ◯◦ 1 Scotland   2 Ireland   3 Poland
> ◦◯ 1 Sudan   2 Iran   3 Iraq

3 (▶7) Ask learners to listen to and practise the words with correct stress and pronunciation.

4 Go over the example and put learners into groups. Tell them to write three questions about countries and capital cities for the other groups.

5 Go over the conversation and tell them that they will get one point for each correct answer, with the winning team being the group with the most points.

6 (▶8) Tell learners to listen and complete the table.

> **Answers**
>
> | name | country | nationality | language(s) |
> |------|---------|-------------|-------------|
> | Hasan | Sudan | Sudanese | Arabic, German |
> | Bangon | Thailand | Thai | Thai |
> | Joanna | Poland | Polish | Polish |
> | Daniel | Romania | Romanian | Romanian |

7 Ask learners to put the words in order to make questions with correct punctuation.

> **Answers**
> 1 Where are you from?
> 2 What's your capital city?
> 3 What's your nationality?
> 4 What's your home town?
> 5 What languages do you speak?

8 (▶9) Ask learners to listen and practise the questions with correct intonation and pronunciation.

9 Ask learners to walk round the class, ask each other the questions and complete the table.

Extension

Ask learners to write as many country names as they can. Then ask them to draw a table with *country – nationality – language* and complete the table.

Answers: Self-study exercises   **Where are you from?**   **Your own notes**

1 Turkey   Turkish   Turkish
  China   Chinese   Chinese
  Iraq   Iraqi   Arabic

2 2 city 3 your 4 What's 5 language(s)

3 Own answers

Where are you from? 2a

1 Label the pictures.

| Iran Iraq Ireland Poland Scotland Sudan |

1 ....
2 ....
3 ....
4 ....
5 ....
6 ....

England
Wales
Egypt
Germany

2 Put the countries into groups.

○ ○ 1 ....Scot land   2 ....   3 ....
○ ○ 1 ....   2 ....   3 ....

3 Listen and practise.

4 Work in groups. Write three questions about countries and capital cities.

What's the capital city of Germany?

5 Ask the other groups your questions.

Group A: What's the capital city of Germany?
Group B: It's Bonn.
Group A: No, that's wrong.
Group C: It's Berlin.
Group A: That's right.

6 Listen to three conversations and complete the table.

name	country	nationality	language(s)
Hasan	Sudan		
Bangon			Thai
Joanna			Polish
Daniel		Romanian	

7 Order the questions.

1 are from you where ....
2 what's capital your city ....
3 nationality your what's ....
4 your what's home town ....
5 languages what do speak you ....

8 Listen and practise.

9 Ask four other learners the questions in exercise 7 and complete the table.

name	country	capital city	nationality	home town	languages

2b I live in a flat

Type of activity
Learners read maps and short texts. Individual and pair work.

AECC reference
Rs/E1.1b, Sc/E1.1b, Sc/E1.3a

Aims
Learners will learn about places in towns, types of housing and prepositions *near*, *next to*, *in* and *on*.

Language
talking about where you live; present simple regular verbs – *live*; prepositions *near*, *next to*, *in* and *on*

Vocabulary
near, *next to*; housing; places in town

Preparation
Photocopy the worksheet. Take a map of your town/city to class.

Differentiation
Weaker learners: write some of the places from exercise 1 on the board, but mix up the letters and ask learners to write the places in order, e.g. *rkap = park*.
Stronger learners: ask them to look at the map and find the full forms for *Ln* (Lane), *Dr* (Drive) and *Sq* (Square).

Warmer

Play 'Hangman' using words for places around town, for example: *bus stop, railway station, park, school*.

1 Ask learners to look at the map and label it with the words. Practise the pronunciation with them.

> **Answers**
> 1 bus stop   2 flats   3 house   4 school
> 5 underground railway station   6 park

2 Tell learners to read the texts and answer the questions.

> **Answers**
> 1 Glasgow   2 a flat   3 Amina
> 4 Maryam   5 with friends

3 Tell learners to look at the pictures and label them with the prepositions.

> **Answers**
> 1 in   2 next to   3 near   4 on

4 Ask learners to look at the map and find the full forms for the abbreviations. Then tell them to write the abbreviations in full with correct spelling.

> **Answers**
> 1 Road   2 Street   3 Lane

5 Ask learners to read the texts again and label the map.

> **Answers**
> A Wei   B Ahmed   C Maryam   D Amina
> E Joanne

6 Tell learners to talk about where they live with a partner.

Extension

Ask learners to look for and write down the places and facilities they have near their homes, and to come back to the class next time and tell other learners.

Answers: Self-study exercises   **I live in a flat**   **Your own notes**

1 1 flat   2 bus stop   3 park   4 school

2 1 in   2 on   3 next to / near   4 on
      5 on, next to / near

3 2 Iraq   3 a flat   4 her mother and father   5 the park

I live in a flat 2b

1 Label the map (1–6).

house   school   underground railway station   park   bus stop   flats

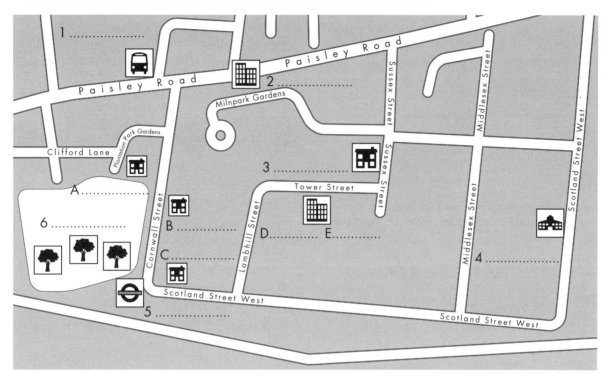

2 Read and answer the questions.

1 Which city does Ahmed live in?
2 Where does Amina live?
3 Who is Joanne's neighbour?

4 Who lives near Ahmed?
5 Who does Wei live with?

- My name's Ahmed. I live in Glasgow in a house on Cornwall Street.
- I'm Amina. I'm from Somalia, but now I live in Glasgow. I live in a flat on Tower Street.
- I'm called Joanne and I'm from Glasgow. I live next to Amina. We live in the same block of flats.
- Ahmed is my friend. I live near Ahmed, near the underground railway station. My name is Maryam.
- My name is Wei. I'm from China. I live with my friends. We live next to the park.

3 Label the pictures.

in   near   next to   on

1 .... 2 .... 3 .... 4 ....

4 Look at the map and write the words in full.

1 Rd ......*Road*...... 2 St .... 3 Ln ....

5 Read again and complete the map (A–E) with the names of the people in exercise 2.

6 Work together. Talk about where you live.

- Where do you live?
- What kind of house do you live in?
- What do you live next to or near?

2c New home

Type of activity
Learners will learn to write addresses and a short text describing where they live.

AECC reference
Wt/E1.1

Aims
To give learners practice in writing with correct punctuation and writing addresses in correct format.

Language
describing people and places; basic adjectives; *we've got*

Vocabulary
terraced house; neighbour; bus station

Preparation
Photocopy the worksheet. Bring in more cards for learners to write on.

Differentiation
Weaker learners: write another address on the board and ask them to cover exercise 1 and label the parts of the address, e.g.
house number – 7 John St – *street name*
Stronger learners: give them more opposites to match such as *large, exciting, safe: small, boring, dangerous.*

Warmer
Write an address on the board with the lines of the address in the wrong order and tell learners to put it into the correct order.

1 Go over the words and make sure they understand them. Ask them to label the address with the words.

> **Answers**
> 1 initials —— A. S. Peto —— 2 last name
> 3 flat/house —— 16–17 Newcombe Rd —— 4 road/street
> number   Handsworth   name
>   Birmingham ——
> 5 area   B21 8DB —— 6 town/city
> 7 postcode   Great Britain —— 8 country

2 Go over the punctuation and practise the pronunciation of the words. Ask learners to match the words with the punctuation.

> **Answers**
> 1 c 2 d 3 a 4 b

3 Ask learners to read the text and answer the questions.

> **Answers**
> 1 in a terraced house in the town centre
> 2 Yes – it's nice and quiet.
> 3 the shops and bus station

4 Go over the adjectives and ask learners to match the opposites. Practise the pronunciation of the words.

> **Answers**
> 1 c 2 d 3 a 4 b

5 Go over the writing template and make sure they understand what to do. Tell learners to use the template to write their own card with address.

Extension
Tell learners to give their card to another learner. Ask the learner to then reply to the card.

Answers: Self-study exercises ••• **New home** ••• **Your own notes**

1 N Parha
121 Lady **M**argaret **R**oad
Southall
Middlesex
UB1 2**NW**

Li Ho
Flat 2
13 **E**dgemont Street
Shawlands
Glasgow
G41 3EH

2 2 unfriendly 3 nice 4 clean

New home 2c

1 Label the address.

area	country	flat/house number
initials	last name	postcode
road/street name	town/city

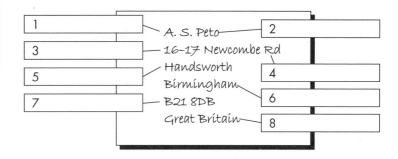

1	
3	A. S. Peto	2
5	16–17 Newcombe Rd	4
7	Handsworth	
	Birmingham	6
	B21 8DB	
	Great Britain	8

2 Match.

1 capital letter   a .
2 comma   b –
3 full stop   c T
4 dash   d ,

3 Read and answer.

1 Where does Erika live?
2 Does Erika like it? Why (not)?
3 Which places are near?

Dear Anna,

We've got a new house in the town centre. It's a terraced house. The area is nice and quiet. Our neighbours are friendly. The shops and the bus station are very near.

Come and see us soon,

Erika

4 Match the opposites.

1 nice   a unfriendly
2 quiet   b dirty
3 friendly   c horrible
4 clean   d noisy

5 Write about your house or flat.

Dear .... ,

We've got a new	house. flat.	It's	near next to

the town centre. the shops. the railway station.	The street is	nice clean quiet

and	the	neighbours people	are	friendly. nice.

Come and	see visit	us soon.

....

3a Can you say that again?

Type of activity
Learners listen to short conversations and match them with pictures, then practise short conversations.

AECC reference
Sc/E1.3d, Lr/E1.1d, Lr/E1.5b

Aims
Learners will learn words for items in class, asking for repetition and using phrases for politeness.

Language
asking for repetition; spelling and clarification; *sorry, excuse me, please, of course, How do you spell ...?, Can you say that again?, What does ... mean?, I don't understand;* affirmative imperatives

Vocabulary
items in class

Preparation
Photocopy the worksheet. Take in classroom objects to pre-teach vocabulary.

Differentiation
Weaker learners: tell them to ask you about the names of more things in the class, e.g. *What's this? It's a door.* Stronger learners: ask them to write another conversation using the phrases for politeness, asking for repetition and classroom items.

Warmer

Play 'I Spy'. Teach learners the phrase: *I spy something beginning with (A)* then show them what to do with one or two things before putting them in groups to play the game with each other.

1 Ask learners to label the items in the picture with the words in the box.

> **Answers**
> 1 desk   2 file   3 rubber   4 board   5 handout
> 6 pencil   7 notebook   8 pen

2 (▶10) Go over the pictures and play the recording. Tell learners to cover up exercise 3 and then to match the conversations with the pictures.

> **Answers**
> picture A conversation 2
> picture B conversation 1
> picture C conversation 3

3 (▶10) Play the recording again and tell learners to complete the conversations.

> **Answers**
> 1 please   2 Excuse me   3 say that   4 of course
> 5 sorry   6 spell   7 understand   8 mean

4 (▶11) Play the recording as learners listen and practise the questions and sentence.

5 Put learners in pairs and ask them to choose one of the conversations and practise it.

Extension

Tell learners they have to use one of the phrases in their daily conversation before the next class then report back and say where and when they used it. Alternatively, if you did the warmer, ask them to play the game with their family at home.

Answers: Self-study exercises   **Can you say that again?**   **Your own notes**

1 1 Open   2 Turn   3 Put

2 2 Excuse   3 mean   4 spell

3 2 I'm sorry   3 of course   4 Thank you

Can you say that again? (3a)

1 Label the picture.

| board desk file handout pen pencil notebook rubber |

1 ....
2 ....
3 ....
4 ....
5 ....
6 ....
7 ....
8 ....

2 Listen and write the conversation number under the picture.

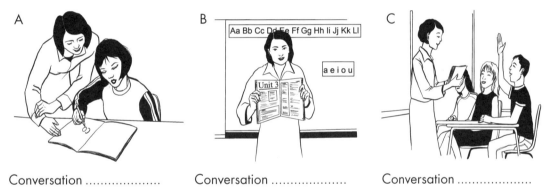

Conversation ....   Conversation ....   Conversation ....

3 Listen again and complete.

| excuse me   mean   of course   please   say that   sorry   spell   understand |

1   Rachel: OK, everyone – it's time to start. Open your books at Unit 3, (1) ....
    Hamad: (2) .... , Rachel, can you (3) .... again, please?
    Rachel: Yes, (4) .... Turn to Unit 3, activity 1.

2   Tharntip: I'm (5) .... , Rachel.
    Rachel: Yes, what is it, Tharntip?
    Tharntip: How do you (6) .... *computer*?
    Rachel: C-O-M-P-U-T-E-R.

3   Rachel: OK, that's all for today then. Put your handouts in your file for the next class.
    Andras: I'm sorry, I don't (7) .... What does *handout* (8) .... ?
    Rachel: A handout is the piece of paper I give you.

4 Listen and practise.

Can you say that again, please?   How do you spell computer?   *I don't understand.*
What does handout *mean?*

5 Work together. Practise a conversation from exercise 3.

3b Class rules

Type of activity
Learners read a short text for instructions about what to do or not to do in college.

AECC reference
Rs/E1.1a, Rt/E1.2

Aims
Learners will practise reading signs and reading for information.

Language
talking about rules; negative imperatives

Vocabulary
class, self-study centre, do (your) homework, rule, mobile phone, litter

Preparation
Photocopy the worksheet. Take in more pictures of signs from around your college.

Differentiation
Weaker learners: ask them to add more sentences to exercise 4, for example *Bring a notebook. Don't leave it at home.*

Stronger learners: ask them to write or say the rules they keep to themselves using *always, never* or *sometimes*: e.g. *I'm always on time for class.*

Warmer
Draw one or two signs for learners on the board (for example, *No smoking, No entry*) and ask them what they mean, then ask learners what other rules they can think of in college.

1 Tell learners to match the signs with the sentences.

> **Answers**
> 1 Do not eat or drink in the classroom.
> 2 Be quiet.
> 3 Turn off your mobile phone.
> 4 Put litter in here.

2 Go over the sentences, then ask them to read the text and tick or cross the rules.

> **Answers**
> 1 ✓ 2 ✓ 3 ✗ 4 ✓ 5 ✗

3 Tell learners to write the contracted forms of the negative verbs.

> **Answers**
> 1 don't 2 aren't 3 doesn't 4 isn't

4 Tell learners to read the text again and write full sentences.

> **Answers**
> 1 Bring a notebook.
> 2 Come to class on time.
> 3 Go to the self-study centre.
> 4 Don't take drinks into class.
> 5 Don't use your mobile phone.

5 Put learners into pairs and ask them to talk about the rules in their college or class. Encourage learners to make positive rules for the class too, for example *Smile in class, Listen to the other learners, Speak in English.*

6 Tell learners to make a poster for their class rules – make sure they include some positive rules too. At the end you could put the posters on the board or round the classroom.

Extension
Ask learners to go round the college and 'collect' (i.e. copy or take photos with their phone if they have one) three more signs they see and write what they think they mean. They could present these at the next class.

Answers: Self-study exercises   **Class rules**   **Your own notes**

1 2 Don't put your litter on the floor.
   3 Don't be late for class.
   4 Don't do another student's homework.
   5 Don't speak your language in class – speak English.

2 2 ✓ 3 ✗ 4 ✗ 5 ✗

Class rules 3b

1 Match.

Be quiet. Do not eat or drink in the classroom. Put litter in here. Turn off your mobile phone.

1 .... 2 .... 3 .... 4 ....

2 Read and tick (✓) the things students do and cross (✗) the things they don't do.

Student handbook – ESOL Entry 1
Welcome to the English course

The Entry 1 course is from 9.30 to 12 and from 1 to 3.30. There are not many rules, but there are some things we ask you to do.

- Bring a pen, notebook and file to class.
- Come to class every day and come on time – don't be late.
- Do your homework – this helps you learn after class.
- Go to the self-study centre after class and ask your teacher for activities to do.
- Don't take food or drinks into class – help us to keep your classroom tidy.

1 ✓ Come every day.
2 ☐ Come to lessons on time.
3 ☐ Forget your pen.
4 ☐ Do your homework.
5 ☐ Take food into class.

3 Write the negatives.

1 do not ....*don't*.... 2 are not .... 3 does not .... 4 is not ....

4 Read again and write full sentences.

1 (✓ bring) a notebook.   *Bring a notebook.*...
2 (✓ come) to class on time.   ....
3 (✓ go) to the self-study centre.   ....
4 (✗ take) drinks into class.   ....
5 (✗ use) your mobile phone.   ....

5 Work together. Say what the rules are in your class.

6 Design a poster for your class with your rules.

CLASS RULES

1 Say 'Hello' to everyone in the class.
2 Don't be late.
3 Do your homework.

3c A note to college

Type of activity
Learners write a short note and learn how to start and finish letters.

AECC reference
Ws/E1.2, Ws/E1.3

Aims
Learners will practise writing short messages, salutations and endings.

Language
apologising; *would like*; *(is it) possible to … ?*

Vocabulary
letter, note, email, envelope, attendance, accommodation

Preparation
Photocopy the worksheet. Take in more (anonymous) letters from learners to the college photocopied onto OHTs for the correction activity in Extension.

Differentiation
Weaker learners: ask them to cover the words in exercise 1 and write them again with correct spelling.
Stronger learners: ask them to write another letter using the phrases in the letters.

Warmer

Ask learners who can spell *Mr*, *Mrs* and *Ms* in full and what they mean. Then ask them who we use *Sir* and *Madam* for. If you have brought in the realia, you could use this first before getting the learners to label the pictures.

1 Ask learners to label the pictures with the words.

> **Answers**
> 1 letter   2 note   3 email   4 envelope

2 Tell learners to read the texts and decide which text is for which person.

> **Answers**
> a 1 and 3   b 2   c 4

3 Ask learners to read the letters again and answer the questions.

> **Answers**
> 1 a Dear Mr ...., / Sir,
>   b Dear Mrs ....,
>   c Dear Sir/Madam,
>
> 2 a Yours,/Thank you,
>   b Yours faithfully,

4 Explain the phrases *I would like, Is it possible*. Show learners that they need to complete the letter by putting the words in order.

> **Answers**
> Dear Mr Davies,
> Is it possible to see you after your class?
> I would like some help with my homework.
> Many thanks,
> (Your name)

Extension

Bring in more letters from learners, making sure that there are no names on them. You could photocopy them onto OHTs. Go over them and ask learners if they can correct any grammar and spelling mistakes.

Answers: Self-study exercises   **A note to college**   **Your own notes**

1 2 letter   3 possible   4 problem   5 office

2 2 would like   3 sorry   4 soon

3 I can't come to your class. I feel ill.

A note to college 3c

1 Label the pictures.

email   envelope   letter   note

32a Woolpark Avenue
Gaywood
King's Lynn

Dear Mrs Harris,

I'm sorry I can't come to class today – my son is ill.

Yours,

Satar

Dear Kim,

Can you give me a letter about my attendance? I would like it for Monday afternoon.

Yours,
Latifa

1 ....

2 ....

Dear Mr Farid,

Is it possible to see you today? I'd like some help with a letter.

Thank you,

Bekele

Dear Sir / Madam,

I would like to see someone about my accommodation problems.

Yours faithfully,

Ali

3 ....

4 ....

2 Read and answer.

Which is for …

a a teacher? (×2)   b a school office?   c a housing office?

3 Answer the questions.

1 How do we start a letter to …
   a a man we know   b a married woman we know   c someone we don't know?

2 How do we finish a letter to
   a someone we know, for example, a teacher   b someone we don't know, for example, an official?

4 Order the letter.

Davies Mr, Dear   _Dear Mr Davies,_.........................

see you it possible ? class after Is to

....

help I like some my homework . would with

....

, thanks Many

....

(Your name)

4a Time

Type of activity
Learners listen to an itinerary and do an information gap activity. Individual and pair work.

AECC reference
Sc/E1.4a, Lr/E1.2c, Lr/E1.4b

Aims
Learners will practise *Wh-* questions, telling the time and making statements of fact clearly.

Language
asking for and giving times; *Wh-* questions, times

Vocabulary
breakfast, lunch, dinner, tea break

Preparation
Photocopy the worksheet.

Differentiation
Weaker learners: ask them to write out the times in full from the times shown in the illustrations in exercise 6. Stronger learners: ask them to write one or two sentences about what time they get up, have breakfast, come to college; what time their class starts, when the break is, what time the class finishes, and so on.

Warmer

Write *morning/afternoon/evening* on the board and ask learners which meals they have at these times.

1 Go over the words and tell them to match the words with the pictures. Practise the pronunciation of the words.

> **Answers**
> 1 breakfast   2 tea break   3 lunch   4 dinner

2 Tell learners to write the times under the pictures. Practise saying the times.

> **Answers**
> 1 seven o'clock   2 eleven o'clock
> 3 half past twelve   4 quarter past six

3 Go over the times and ask them to match them. Practise saying the times with the learners.

> **Answers**
> 1 c   2 d   3 e   4 b   5 a

4 (▶12) Play the recording and ask learners to write the times.

> **Answers**
> 1 3.10   2 7.45   3 2.25   4 5.40   5 4.55

5 (▶12) Play the recording again and learners say the times.

6 Put the learners into pairs. Tell Student A to cover the section for Student B and Student B to cover the section for Student A. Tell Student A to say the times for Student B to write down in their notebook. When Student A has finished, then Student B should say the times for Student A to write in their notebook.

> **Answers**
> 1 five o'clock   2 half past three   3 quarter to nine
> 4 five past one   5 twenty to eight
> 6 quarter past eleven

7 (▶13) Tell learners to listen to the recording and tick the times they hear.

> **Answers**
> 1 7.00   2 12.30   3 6.15

8 (▶14) Play the recording and tell learners to practise the questions.

9 Put the learners into groups and ask them to ask each other what time they have different meals.

Extension

Ask learners to walk around and ask their classmates *When is your bus home?*, *What time is your first class on Monday?*, *When is your last class on Friday?*, etc.

Answers: Self-study exercises   Time

1 2 half past eleven   3 quarter to twelve
4 ten past three   5 twenty to seven

2 2 What time do you have lunch?
3 When is the break?

3 2 when   3 twelve thirty   4 what time

Your own notes

1 Match.

| breakfast   dinner   lunch   tea break |

1 ....
....

2 ....
....

3 ....
....

4 ....
....

2 Write the times under the pictures.

| eleven o'clock   quarter past six   half past twelve   seven o'clock |

3 Match the times.

1 six fifteen   a ten to nine
2 five thirty   b quarter to twelve
3 four twenty-five   c quarter past six
4 eleven forty-five   d half past five
5 eight fifty   e twenty-five past four

4 Listen and write the times.

1 ...._3.10_....   2 ....   3 ....   4 ....   5 ....

5 Listen again and practise.

6 Work in pairs. Say and write the time.

7 Listen to a conversation and tick (✓).

1 Breakfast: 7.00 ☐   7.30 ☐

2 Lunch: 12.05 ☐   12.30 ☐

3 Dinner   6.15 ☐   5.45 ☐

8 Listen and practise the questions.

What time do you have (breakfast)?   *When is (lunch)?*

9 Ask classmates what time they have breakfast, lunch and dinner.

name				
breakfast				
lunch				
dinner				

From *ESOL Activities Entry 1* © Cambridge University Press 2008   **PHOTOCOPIABLE**   (29)

4b College trip

Type of activity
Learners read a poster about a school trip to obtain information, and practise asking questions to complete an information gap activity. Individual and pair work.

AECC reference
Rs/E1.1a, Rt/E1.1b, Sc/E1.4a

Aims
Learners will practise *Wh-* questions with the present simple, telling the time and reading texts to obtain factual information.

Language
saying months; present simple questions with third person plural; prepositions *at* and *in*

Vocabulary
trip, beautiful, lovely, lake, sea, palace, royal, leave, arrive, end

Preparation
Photocopy the worksheet.

Differentiation
Weaker learners: give them the short forms of the months (*Jan, Feb …*) and ask them to write them in full.
Stronger learners: ask them to make a list of tourist attractions in their own country and to write short descriptions of what they are and why they are good to visit.

Warmer
Play 'Hangman' with words like *castle, palace, lake* and *sea* or other words associated with places to visit.

1 Revise months of the year and ask learners to put them in order.

> **Answers**
> 1 January   2 February   3 March   4 April   5 May
> 6 June   7 July   8 August   9 September
> 10 October   11 November   12 December

2 Tell learners to read the poster and answer the questions.

> **Answers**
> 1 Yes
> 2 No – the trip is to Leeds Castle
> 3 No – it ends at 1.00

3 Tell learners to read the next poster and answer the questions.

> **Answers**
> 1 8.30   2 10.00   3 3.00

4 Split the class into Student A and Student B and tell them to write questions about the posters.

> **Answers**
> **Student A:**
> 1 What time do the students leave London?
> 2 When do they arrive at Leeds Castle?
> 3 What time do they arrive in London?
> **Student B:**
> 1 What time do the students have lunch?
> 2 What time do they visit the Royal Pavilion?
> 3 When do they arrive in London?

5 Put learners into pairs: Student A and Student B. Tell them to ask each other the questions and to answer them by reading the posters again.

> **Answers**
> **Student A:** 1 9.00   2 10.00   3 3.00
> **Student B:** 1 12.00   2 1.15   3 4.30

Extension
Ask learners to find out about a local tourist attraction, in particular the days it is open and the opening and closing times.

Answers: Self-study exercises   College trip   **Your own notes**

1 2 at   3 at   4 in
2 2 5.45
    3 10.00, 10.00 pm / 22.00
    4 closed

College trip 4b

1 Put the months in order.

| April | August | December | February | January | June |
| July | March | May | November | October | September |

1 .... 4 .... 7 .... 10 ....

2 .... 5 .... 8 .... 11 ....

3 .... 6 .... 9 .... 12 ....

2 Read and write Yes or No.

1 Does the bus leave from London? .... 3 Is lunch at one o'clock? ....

2 Is the trip to Lee Castle? .... 4 Does the visit end at two o'clock? ....

TRIP TO LEEDS CASTLE
Saturday 4th June

Leeds Castle is a beautiful castle in the middle of a lake.

Leave London: 9.00

Arrive Leeds Castle: 10.00

End visit: 1.00

Lunch: 1.00 – 2.00

Arrive London: 3.00

3 Read and answer.

1 What time do the students leave London?

2 When do they arrive in Brighton?

3 What time do they visit the Royal Pavilion?

4 When do the students leave Brighton?

TRIP TO BRIGHTON
Sunday 7th July

Brighton is a lovely city next to the sea with a royal pavilion.

Leave London: 8.30

Arrive Brighton: 10.00

Lunch: 12.00

Visit Brighton Royal Pavilion: 1.15

Leave Brighton: 3.00

Arrive London: 4.30

4 Student A, write questions about the trip to Leeds Castle.
Student B, write questions about the trip to Brighton.

Student A

1 What time / the students / London? ....

2 When / they / at Leeds Castle? ....

3 What / do they / in London? ....

Student B

1 What time / the students / lunch? ....

2 What time / the Royal Pavilion? ....

3 When / they / in London? ....

5 Work together. Ask each other questions about the trips. Read the posters and answer the questions.

4c) A visit

Type of activity
Learners write a letter to go on a school trip and make a poster for a school trip to a place nearby. Individual and group work.

AECC reference
Ws/E1.1

Aims
Learners will learn to construct a simple sentence and learn the format of a simple letter.

Language
saying dates; *would like*

Vocabulary
ordinal numbers; *visit*

Preparation
Photocopy the worksheet. Take in a map of the UK or photos of local cities to visit. Make Bingo cards with dates on them for the warmer.

Differentiation
Weaker learners: write out some more dates and tell them to write them in full, e.g. *9th Feb – the ninth of February.*
Stronger learners: ask them to correct some dates, e.g. *the ten of March, the second of the June.*

Warmer

Make some Bingo cards using dates, for example:

2 /11	5/06	3/12
4/01	2/7	8/02

Revise numbers and months and show learners how we say dates. Show them how to play Bingo. Read out the dates as learners listen and cross them out on their Bingo cards. The learner who crosses out all the dates on their card first should shout *Bingo!* and is the winner.

1 Tell learners to put the dates in order.

> **Answers**
> a 2   b 1   c 4   d 3   e 5

2 Ask learners to write the dates in full.

> **Answers**
> 1 the fifth of January   2 the eighth of July
> 3 the third of August   4 the first of September
> 5 the second of December

3 Tell learners to read the letters and complete the table.

> **Answers**
> 1 Edinburgh
> 2 the eighth of July
> 3 the fourth of April

4 Ask learners to read the letters again and answer the questions.

> **Answers**
> 1 Her children and a friend
> 2 Ahmed and Rahim, and Zakir
> 3 Their wives (Ahmed and Rahim); his son (Zakir)

5 Go over the words then ask them to complete the letter.

> **Answers**
> 1 Toni   2 would like   3 bring   4 my   5 Yours

6 Put learners in groups and ask them to design a poster for a trip to a place near the college. You could refer them back to the posters in 4b for ideas. Put the posters on the wall and tell learners to look at them and decide which trip they would like to go on.

7 Tell learners to write a letter asking for a place on the trip to the place on the poster they liked.

Extension

Ask learners to make another poster, this time about a tourist attraction in their home country.

---

1 2 I would like to go on the trip.
   3 I would like to bring my children.
   4 We would like to visit Manchester.

2

> Date ....
> Dear _____ ,
> We would like to go on the college trip to London.
> I would like to bring my two friends.
> Yours,
> _____

A visit (4c)

1 Put the dates in order.

a 8th July ....   c 1st September ....   e 2nd December ....
b 5th January ....1....   d 3rd August ....

2 Write the dates in full.

the fifth of January

3 Read and complete.

date	place
the twelfth of January	1 ....
2	York
3	Bath

Thursday 1st April

Dear Toni,
We would like to go on the college trip to Bath on 4th April. We - Rahim and I - would like to bring our wives.

Yours,
Ahmed and Rahim

Tuesday 8th July

Dear Tutor,
I would like to go on the visit to York on 1st August. I would like to bring my two children and a friend.

Yours,
Serap Hanci

Wednesday 8th January

Dear Teacher,
I would like to join the college trip to Edinburgh on 12th January. I would like to bring my son.

Thanks,
Zakir

4 Read and answer.

1 Who does Serap want to bring?   2 Who are the other letters from?   3 Who do they want to bring?

5 Complete the letter.

bring   my   Toni   would like   Yours

6 Work in groups. Make a poster for a visit to a place near you.

7 Look at the posters. Decide where you would like to go. Write a letter saying you would like to go on the trip.

Wednesday 30th July

Dear (1) .... ,
I (2) .... to go on the visit to Brighton. I want to (3) .... my children and (4) .... wife.

(5) .... ,
Ahmed

5a Morning

Type of activity
Learners listen to someone talking about their morning routine. Individual and class work.

AECC reference
Sc/E1.4a, Lr/E1.2c, Lr/E1.4b

Aims
Learners will practise talking about routines.

Language
talking about routines; present simple first person and *yes/no* questions; short answers

Vocabulary
wake up, get out (of bed), wash, brush, have a shower, make (breakfast), drink, say goodbye to, close, early

Preparation
Photocopy the worksheet. You could bring in a few items for exercise 2 (e.g. towel, soap, toothbrush, cup, kettle) to demonstrate how to mime/perform the actions.

Differentiation
Weaker learners: tell them to cover exercise 1 when they have finished it, then dictate the phrases to them and tell them to write them down.
Stronger learners: ask them to write a few sentences about another learner, taking care with any negative third person sentences: e.g. *Ala doesn't wake up early.*

Warmer
Ask learners what time they get up and what they do in the morning.

1 Go over the phrases and ask learners to label the pictures.

> **Answers**
> 1 wake up   2 get out of bed   3 wash your face
> 4 brush your teeth   5 have a shower
> 6 make breakfast   7 drink your tea   8 say
> goodbye to everyone   9 close the door

2 (▶15) Tell learners to listen and perform the actions.

3 (▶16) Ask learners to listen to an interview and complete the table with Yes or No.

> **Answers**
> 1 Yes   2 Yes   3 Yes   4 Yes   5 Yes   6 No

4 (▶16) Play the recording again. Tell learners to cover up exercise 3 and then to listen and complete the questions.

> **Answers**
> 1 Do you wake up early?
> 2 Do you have a shower in the morning?
> 3 Do you make breakfast?
> 4 Do you get the children ready?
> 5 Do you go to college?
> 6 Do you do your homework in the morning?

5 (▶17) Play the recording and practise the questions.

6 (▶18) Play the recording and practise the questions and answers.

7 Tell learners to ask three classmates the questions and note down the answers. At the end of the exercise you could put all their answers on the board.

Extension
Tell learners to ask their friends and family what they do in the morning and write a short paragraph about this. Alternatively, you could ask learners to write about the class survey in exercise 7 using *Everyone ... ; Some learners ...; No one ... .*

Answers: Self-study exercises	Morning	Your own notes

1 2 get   3 have   4 brush   5 make   6 drink   7 say
8 close

2 Learners' own answers

Morning (5a)

1 Label the pictures.

| brush your teeth close the door drink your tea get out of bed have a shower |
| make breakfast say goodbye to everyone wake up wash your face |

1 .... 2 .... 3 .... 4 .... 5 ....

6 .... 7 .... 8 .... 9 ....

2 Listen and do the actions.

3 Listen to an interview and write Yes or No.

How busy is your morning?				
Do you ...	name	1	2	3
	Ala			
1 wake up early?	Yes			
2 have a shower?				
3 make breakfast?				
4 get the children ready?				
5 go to college?				
6 do your homework?				

4 Listen again and complete the questions.

1 .... you wake up early?
2 Do you .... a shower in the morning?
3 Do you .... breakfast?
4 .... you get the children ready?
5 Do you .... to college?
6 Do you do your .... in the morning?

5 Listen and practise the questions.

6 Listen and practise the questions and answers.

Do you make breakfast?   Yes, I do.
Do you do your homework in the morning?   No, I don't.

7 Ask three more learners the questions in exercise 4 and write their answers in the table in exercise 3.

5b My family

Type of activity
Learners read a text about a family and complete a family tree. Individual, pair work.

AECC reference
Rs/E1.1a, Rt/E1.1a, Sc/E1.3b

Aims
Learners will practise reading for specific and general information.

Language
talking about your family; *have got*; possessives

Vocabulary
mum, dad, sister, brother, son, daughter

Preparation
Photocopy the worksheet. Take in a copy of your own family tree.

Note: this may be a sensitive area for some learners, so make sure that none of your learners will be upset by the topic.

Differentiation
Weaker learners: ask them to write out the formal versions of *mum, dad, kids, grandad, grandma*. Stronger learners: ask them to rewrite the sentences in exercise 3 to make them true. (1 Marta has two children. 2 They live in London. 3 Marta's husband is Polish. 5 Marek is 22.).

Warmer
Ask learners if they know what the everyday/colloquial English is for *mother* (*mum*), *father* (*dad*) and *children* (*kids*). You could extend this to *grandfather* and *grandmother*.

1 Go over the words, making sure learners understand them. Practise the pronunciation of the words. Tell learners to label the picture.

> **Answers**
> 1 mum   2 dad   3 sister   4 son

2 Go over the family tree. Tell learners to read the text and complete it.

> **Answers**
> 1 Adam   2 daughter's   3 two   4 brother   5 Irena
> 6 22

3 Ask learners to read the text again and answer true or false.

> **Answers**
> 1 False   2 False   3 False   4 True   5 False

4 Tell learners to put possessive 's into the sentences.

> **Answers**
> 1 Marta is Adam's wife.
> 2 Jozef is Adam's son.
> 3 Marta's brother's name is Marek.

5 Ask learners to draw their family tree. You may want to teach more family vocabulary at this point.

6 Practise the questions. Put learners in pairs and tell them to draw each other's family tree by asking and answering questions.

Extension
Tell learners to write one or two sentences about their family.

Answers: Self-study exercises   **My family**   **Your own notes**

1 2 your   3 his   4 her   5 its   6 our   7 their

2 1 Jane   2 Karl   3 Barbara

My family 5b

1 Label the picture.

| dad | mum | sister | son |

1 ....   2 ....

3 daughter/....................   4 ..../brother

2 Look at the family tree. Read and complete.

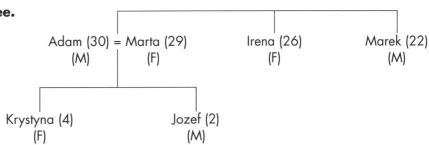

Adam (30) = Marta (29)   Irena (26)   Marek (22)
(M)   (F)   (F)   (M)

Krystyna (4)   Jozef (2)
(F)   (M)

My family

My name is Marta. I'm 29 and I'm married. My husband's name is
(1) .... We've got two children: one girl and one boy. Our
(2) .... name is Krystyna and our son is called Jozef. Krystyna is
four and Jozef is only (3) .... We live in London but we are Polish.
My husband is from Warsaw. He's 30 years old. At home we speak Polish,
but we speak English at work and school. I've got one sister and one
(4) .... My sister's name is (5) .... She lives in Krakow
and she is 26 years old. Her husband is a teacher. My brother's name is
Marek. He's (6) .... and he's a student.

3 Read again and write True or False.

1 Marta's got four children. ....
2 They live in Madrid. ....
3 Marta's husband is British. ....
4 Marta's sister lives in Krakow. ....
5 Marek is 26. ....

4 Write with 's.

1 Marta is Adams wife.   2 Jozef is Adams son.   3 Martas brothers name is Marek.

5 Draw your family tree.

6 Work together. Ask your partner about their family. Ask ...

What's your name?   *How old are you?*   *Are you married?*   *Have you got any children?*
Have you got any brothers or sisters?   *How old are they?*

5c Julia's day

Type of activity
Learners complete a short text about their daily life.
Individual, pair work.

AECC reference
Ws/E1.3, Ww/E1.1c

Aims
Learners will practise writing a short text about someone's day.

Language
asking for information; present simple third person

Vocabulary
domestic chores: *wash up, do the washing, tidy up, cook, do the shopping, clean, make the bed*

Preparation
Photocopy the worksheet.

Differentiation
Weaker learners: give them more common verbs and ask them to write them with the third person ending.
Stronger learners: ask them to make a list of more jobs in the house, for example *hoover, sweep the floor, dust*.

Warmer

Put learners into groups and dictate some common verbs to them: *wash, clean, carry, cook*. For each correctly spelled word, award one point. The group with the most correctly spelled words is the winner.

1 Tell learners to label the pictures with the words and phrases. Practise the pronunciation of the words and phrases.

> **Answers**
> 1 wash up   2 do the washing   3 tidy up   4 cook
> 5 do the shopping   6 clean   7 make the bed

2 Tell learners to read the text and complete it using the pictures.

> **Answers**
> 1 makes the beds   2 tidies up   3 walks
> 4 does the shopping   5 does the washing
> 6 cooks   7 watches

3 (▶19) Play the recording as learners listen and read the text.

4 Ask learners to put the verbs from the text into groups.

> **Answers**
> 1 cleans, cooks, makes, meets, talks, walks
> 2 does, washes, watches
> 3 carries, tidies

5 Ask learners to read the text again and answer the questions.

> **Answers**
> 1 seven o'clock   2 in the town centre   3 her friend
> 4 plays with her children, talks to her husband, watches TV

6 Tell learners to use the words to write questions.

> **Answers**
> 1 What time do you get up?
> 2 What do you do in the morning?
> 3 What do you do in the afternoon?
> 4 What do you do in the evening?

7 Practise the questions then put learners in pairs. Ask them to ask each other the questions.

8 Ask learners to write three or four sentences about their partner's day using the prompts to guide them.

Extension

Ask learners to write one or two sentences about their partner's day or another person's day.

Answers: Self-study exercises   **Julia's day**   **Your own notes**

1 2 do the washing   3 tidy up   4 cook   5 do the shopping   6 clean   7 make the bed

2 2 tidies up   3 walks   4 does the shopping
5 cooks   6 watches

Julia's day (5c)

1 Match the words with the pictures.

| clean   cook   do the shopping   do the washing   make the bed   tidy up   wash up |

1 ....
2 ....
3 ....
4 ....

5 ....
6 ....
7 ....

2 Complete the text.

A day in Julia's life

Julia wakes up at seven o'clock. She makes breakfast and takes the children to school.

She (1) .... , washes up and (2) .... At ten o'clock Julia

(3) .... to the town centre, (4) .... and carries

the bags home. She meets her friend for lunch. In the afternoon she cleans and

(5) .... Then she (6) .... dinner. In the evening Julia

plays with her children and talks to her husband, and then she (7) .... TV.

3 Listen and check.

4 Put into groups.

| carry   ~~clean~~   cook   do   make   meet   talk   tidy   walk   wash   watch |

1 +s: ...... *cleans* ....
2 +es: ....
3 +ies: ....

5 Read again and answer.

1 What time does Julia wake up? ....
2 Where does she shop for food? ....

3 Who does she meet for lunch? ....
4 What does she do in the evening? ....

6 Write questions.

1 / time / you get up? ....
2 What / you / in the morning? ....

3 What / you / in the afternoon? ....
4 / you do / the evening? ....

7 Work together. Ask each other the questions.

8 Write about your friend or partner's day.

In the morning (Ahmed) ...   In the afternoon (he) ...   In the evening (he) ...

6a At the market

Type of activity
Learners listen to a conversation and do a dictation activity then practise the conversation. Individual and pair work.

AECC reference
Sc/E1.2a, Le/E1.1c, Lr/E1.2e

Aims
Learners will practise making requests and asking questions to obtain information in a familiar context.

Language
making requests; questions with *How much … ?*; countable nouns

Vocabulary
fruit and vegetables

Preparation
Photocopy the worksheet. Take in assorted fruit and vegetables.

Differentiation
Weaker learners: ask them to write in full and practise the pronunciation of more prices and weights.
Stronger learners: ask them to say where they go shopping and what they buy.

Warmer

Write *Vegetables/Fruit* on the board, put learners in groups and tell them to write as many of the items they can think of. The group with the most correct items is the winner.

1 Ask learners to label the picture. If you have brought in some fruit and vegetables, use these to pre-teach and practise the vocabulary. Practise the pronunciation of the words with learners.

> **Answers**
> 1 bananas   2 pears   3 onions   4 peppers
> 5 carrots

2 (▶20) Ask learners to listen and practise the pronunciation of the prices.

3 Tell learners to look at the picture for a minute and then cover it. Then they try to answer the questions.

> **Answers**
> 1 Yes, they do.   2 No, they don't.   3 50p a kilo
> 4 40p a kilo   5 32p a kilo

4 Tell learners to use the cues to write three more questions about the picture.

> **Answers**
> 1 Do you have any onions?
> 2 How much are the strawberries?
> 3 How much are the bananas?

5 Put learners into pairs and tell them to ask each other the questions from exercise 4.

6 (▶21) Tell learners to cover up exercise 7. Listen to the conversation and tick the items the woman buys.

> **Answers**
> She buys: potatoes (two kilos); tomatoes (one kilo); onions (one and a half kilos)

7 (▶21) Play the conversation again and ask learners to listen and complete the conversation. Point out the use of *love* and ask them if they know any other informal ways of addressing people.

> **Answers**
> 1 two kilos   2 Here you are   3 a half   4 that
> 5 altogether

8 Put learners in pairs and ask them to practise the conversation.

Extension

Ask learners to go round the market or supermarket in their area and collect the prices of a limited number of fruit and vegetables, so that they find the cheapest place to shop for these.

Answers: Self-study exercises   **At the market**   **Your own notes**

1 2 Do you have any bananas?
  3 How much is that?

2 2 want   3 here   4 OK   5 How much   6 altogether

At the market 6a

1 Label the picture.

| bananas carrots onions pears peppers |

1 ....
2 ....
3 ....
4 ....
5 ....

2 Listen and say the prices.

3 Look at the picture for one minute and answer the questions.

1 Do they have any tomatoes? ....
2 Do they have any pineapples? ....
3 How much are the peppers? ....
4 How much are the pears? ....
5 How much are the oranges? ....

4 Write three more questions.

1 Do they / any ? ....

2 How / are the ....

3 How much / the ....

5 Ask each other the questions.

6 Listen and tick (✓) the things in exercise 1 the woman buys.

7 Listen and complete the conversation.

| a half   that   a kilo   here you are   altogether |

Seller: Hello, love, what can I get you today?
Jolanta: Let me think. I want two kilos of potatoes.
Seller: Two kilos of potatoes. (1) ....
Jolanta: And (2) .... of tomatoes.
Seller: OK.
Jolanta: And one and (3) .... kilos of onions.
Seller: Here you are.
Jolanta: Thanks. How much is (4) .... ?
Seller: Two pounds sixteen (5) .... , please.

8 Work together. Practise the conversation.

6b Going shopping

Type of activity
Learners read a short text then work together to complete the information. Individual and pair work.

AECC reference
Rt/E1.1b, Rw/E1.3b, Sc/E1.3b

Aims
Learners will practise obtaining information from texts and recognising digits.

Language
asking for information; *Wh-* questions; large numbers: *hundred, thousand, million*

Vocabulary
shopping centre, restaurant, cinema, car park, stall, shop, escalator, lift, toilets

Preparation
Photocopy the worksheet. Take in brochures for local shopping areas or markets.

Differentiation
Weaker learners: ask them to write in full *100, 1,000, 1,000,000*.
Stronger learners: ask them to write more questions about the text, for example *How many people visit the Trafford Centre?*, *What is the eating area called?*, *What can you buy at Longsight Market?*

Warmer

Ask learners the names of any shopping centres, supermarkets or markets in their area that they know.

1 Go over the words and practise the pronunciation. Then ask them to label the plan with the words.

> **Answers**
> 1 lift   2 telephone   3 car park   4 escalator
> 5 toilets

2 Split the class into A/B pairs and ask them to read their texts and complete their table.

> **Answers**
> Student A
>
> | name | place | number of shops | parking spaces | opening times |
> |------|-------|-----------------|----------------|---------------|
> | The Trafford Centre | 5 miles from Manchester city centre | 230 | 10,000 | Monday – Friday 10 am – 10 pm; Sunday 12 – 6 pm |
>
> Student B
>
> | name | place | number of shops | parking spaces | opening times |
> |------|-------|-----------------|----------------|---------------|
> | Longsight Market | Manchester | over 100 | 50 | Wednesdays and Fridays 9 am – 4.30 pm; Saturdays 9am – 5 pm |

3 (▶22) Play the recording and ask learners to practise saying large numbers.

4 Go over the table headings and ask learners to complete the questions.

> **Answers**
> 1 Where is Longsight Market / the Trafford Centre?
> 2 When is it open?
> 3 How many shops are there?
> 4 How many parking spaces are there?

5 Put learners in pairs and tell them to ask each other their questions to complete the tables.

> **Answers**
> See exercise 2

Extension

Ask learners to complete the table for a local shopping centre or a very large shopping centre like Meadowhall (http://www.meadowhall.co.uk/) or Bluewater (http://www.bluewater.co.uk).

Answers: Self-study exercises   **Going shopping**   **Your own notes**

1 1 restaurants   2 cinema   3 car park   4 shops

2 2 two hundred and thirty
3 ten thousand
4 thirty million

3 2 thirty six
3 ten thousand
4 Thirty million

Going shopping 6b

1 Label.

| car park |
| escalator |
| lift |
| telephone |
| toilets |

1 ....
3 ....

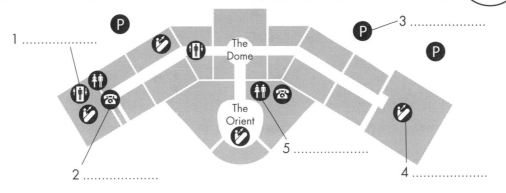

The Dome

The Orient

2 ....
5 ....
4 ....

2 Work together. Student A, read about the Trafford Centre. Complete your table.

The Trafford Centre

The Trafford Centre has 30 million visitors a year. It is five miles from Manchester city centre. The shopping centre has 230 shops. The shopping centre's eating area – The Orient – has 36 restaurants. It has a cinema and 10,000 free car parking spaces. Shops are open Monday to Friday 10 am – 10 pm, and Sunday 12 – 6 pm.

name	place	number of shops	parking spaces	opening times
			10,000	

Student B. Read about Longsight Market. Complete your table

Longsight Market

Longsight Market is a small, friendly market in Manchester. You can buy things for your house, clothes, fresh meat, vegetables and herbs. There are over 100 stalls and shops. There are 50 spaces for cars. The market is open on Wednesdays and Fridays 9 am – 4.30 pm, and Saturdays 9 am – 5 pm.

name	place	number of shops	parking spaces	opening times

3 Listen and practise the numbers.

100   230   10,000   30,000,000

4 Complete the questions about the table.

1 Where is … ?   *Where is Longsight Market / the Trafford Centre?* ....
2 When is … open?   ....
3 How many … are there?   ....
4 How many … are there?   ....

5 Work together. Ask each other questions and complete the table.

Student A

name	place	number of shops	parking spaces	opening times
Longsight Market				

Student B

name	place	number of shops	parking spaces	opening times
Trafford Centre				

6c A shopping list

Type of activity
Learners read and write short notes and lists. Individual and pair work.

AECC reference
Ww/E1.1c

Aims
Learners will practise constructing simple sentences and writing a simple text to communicate ideas.

Language
writing reminders; containers and determiners of quantity; *remember to; don't forget to*

Vocabulary
a kilo, a bag, a packet, a jar, a bottle, a litre, a loaf, a box, a bunch

Preparation
Photocopy the worksheet. Take in food containers such as boxes, bags, packets.

Differentiation
Weaker learners: ask them to cover the words in exercise 1 and write them again with correct spelling.
Stronger learners: ask them to think of more things that come in jars, packets, boxes, bunches and so on.

Warmer

Play 'Odd one out' with some of the words in exercise 1, for example:
coffee   milk   litre   cola
biscuits   packet   crisps   bread
strawberries   kiwi fruit   oranges   bag

1 Ask learners to label the pictures. Then practise the pronunciation of the words. If you brought in more containers, you could use them to pre-teach some of the vocabulary.

> **Answers**
> 1 a kilo   2 a box   3 a bag   4 a packet   5 a jar
> 6 a litre   7 a loaf   8 a bunch

2 Ask learners to make plural forms from the words. Point out the spelling rule of adding *-s* to make most plurals, but adding *-es* to words ending *-s, -sh, -ch* and *-x*, and irregular plurals like *loaves, women, children*.

> **Answers**
> 1 kilos   2 packets   3 boxes   4 bunches   5 loaves

3 Tell learners to read the texts and answer the questions.

> **Answers**
> 1 Claire   2 Trish   3 Valerie   4 Neil

4 Tell learners to read the notes again and complete them, taking care with plural forms.

> **Answers**
> 1 litre   2 loaves   3 bunch   4 boxes

5 Go over the shopping list and then tell learners to write a note for someone, using the writing framework.

Extension

Ask learners to write their own shopping list and then pass it to another learner.

Answers: Self-study exercises   **A shopping list**   **Your own notes**

1 2 a box of chocolates
3 a bag of sugar
4 a bottle of milk

2 2 a bottle of milk
3 a jar of coffee
4 two bottles of cola
5 four bags of crisps

A shopping list 6c

1 Label the pictures.

| a bag | a box | a bunch | a jar | a kilo | a litre | a loaf | a packet |

1 .... 2 .... 3 .... 4 ....

5 .... 6 .... 7 .... 8 ....

2 Make plurals.

1 a kilo – two ......*kilos*......   3 a box – four ....   5 a loaf – three ....

2 a packet – two ....   4 a bunch – two ....

3 Read the notes and answer the questions.

Who would like

1 tissues?   2 coffee?   3 bread?   4 flowers?

Dear Maria,
When you go to the shops, don't forget to buy ...
a (1) .... of milk
a jar of coffee
three packets of crisps
Thanks, Trish

Maria,
Please bring one bottle of washing-up liquid and remember to buy two
(2) .... of bread!
Valerie

Maria,
Just a reminder ... can you buy a
(3) .... of flowers when you go to the shops?
Neil

Dear Maria,
Remember to get a kilo of onions, three
(4) .... of tissues and 2½ kilos of potatoes from the shops.
Claire

4 Read again and complete the notes.

| boxes | bunch | litre | loaves |

5 Read the shopping list and write a note.

Shopping list
eggs (1 box)
lamb (1 kg)
orange juice (2 l)
parsley (1 bunch)
sugar (2 bags)

(Dear) .... ,

| Remember to Don't forget to Please | buy get bring | a | kilo litre bag box | of | flour milk sugar tissues | when you go to from | the shop(s). the supermarket. the market. |

Thanks, ...

7a) Welcome

Type of activity

Learners listen to a conversation and practise phrases for complimenting and welcoming people. Individual and pair work.

AECC reference

Sd/E1.1a, Lr/E1.1a, Lr/E1.2b

Aims

Learners will practise taking part in simple social interaction.

Language

greeting and offering; *What a (nice) ... !; Come in*

Vocabulary

rooms in a house; *relax*

Preparation

Photocopy the worksheet.

Differentiation

Weaker learners: ask them to cover the words in exercise 1 and write them again with correct spelling.
Stronger learners: ask them to write a similar conversation to the one in exercise 4, using some of the phrases in it.

Warmer

Put learners into groups and ask them to think of as many rooms in the house as they can in two minutes. The group with the most rooms is the winner.

1 Tell learners to label the picture and then practise the pronunciation of the words.

> **Answers**
> 1 living room   2 dining room   3 kitchen   4 hall
> 5 bedroom   6 bathroom

2 Tell one or two learners to use the phrases to make sentences, and then ask the class to make sentences with the words in exercises 1 and 2.

> **Answers**
> 1 We eat in the dining room.
> 2 We keep our coats in the hall.
> 3 We have a shower in the bathroom.
> 4 We relax in the living room.
> 5 We sleep in the bedroom.
> 6 We watch TV in the living room.

3 (▶23) Play the recording and tell learners to practise the words and sentences.

4 (▶24) Tell learners to cover up exercise 5. Play the recording and tell learners to listen and tick the rooms they hear.

> **Answers**
> living room ✓ kitchen ✓ bedroom ✓ bathroom ✓

5 Ask learners to try to complete the conversation with the phrases.

6 (▶24) Play the recording again and tell learners to check their answers to exercise 5.

> **Answers**
> 1 Come in
> 2 show you around
> 3 What a lovely house

7 (▶25) Play the recording and tell learners to practise the phrases.

8 Tell them to practise the conversation in exercise 5 using their own names. Ask them to stand up and perform the conversation as they say it.

Extension

Give learners some Post-it® notes and ask them to write the names of the rooms on them. Tell them to stick them on the doors of the rooms at home and learn them for next class.

Answers: Self-study exercises   **Welcome**   **Your own notes**

1 2 We have a shower in the bathroom.
3 We eat dinner in the dining room.
4 We watch TV in the living room.

2 2 What a lovely house
3 show you around
4 Upstairs
5 really nice

Welcome 7a

1 Label the picture.

| bathroom   bedroom   dining room   hall   kitchen   living room |

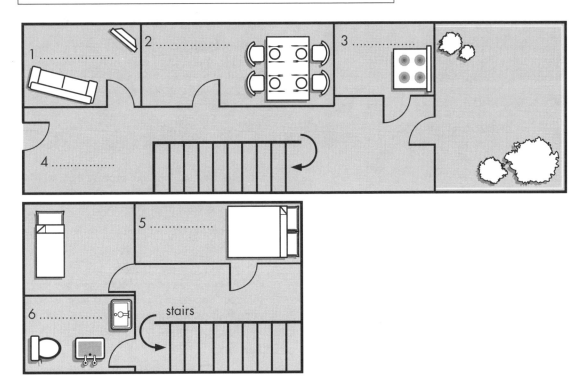

2 Make sentences with the words in exercises 1 and 2.

| ~~cook meals~~   eat   keep our coats   have a shower   relax   sleep   watch TV |

We cook meals in the kitchen.

3 Listen and practise.

4 Listen to a conversation. Tick (✓) the rooms in exercise 1 you hear.

5 Complete the conversation.

| show you around   come in   what a lovely house |

  Julia: Hello, Jemma. (1) ....
Jemma: Thanks, Julia.
  Julia: Let me (2) .... The living room is here on the left.
Jemma: What a nice room!
  Julia: The kitchen is next to the living room. Upstairs there are two bedrooms and a bathroom.
Jemma: (3) .... ! It's a really nice place.
  Julia: Thank you.

6 Listen again and check.

7 Listen and practise the sentences.

Come in.   Let me show you around.   What a lovely house!   It's a really nice place.

8 Work together. Practise the conversation in exercise 5.

7b A flat to rent

Type of activity
Learners read an estate agent's description and do an information gap activity. Individual and pair work.

AECC reference
Rt/E1.1b, Sc/E1.4a, Lr/E1.2e

Aims
Learners will practise reading and obtaining information from texts.

Language
describing your room; prepositions *next to, under, to the left/right of, in the middle of, opposite*

Vocabulary
sofa, wardrobe, cooker, radiator, fridge, shower, bath, sink, double bed

Preparation
Photocopy the worksheet.

Differentiation
Weaker learners: dictate some of the vocabulary in exercise 1 and ask them to spell it correctly.
Stronger learners: ask them to write a short description of one of their rooms.

Warmer

Ask learners what the difference is between *For Sale* and *To Let*. Ask them what *furniture* means and tell them to brainstorm in two minutes the items of furniture they know.

1 Tell learners to look at the picture and label the items. Practise the pronunciation of the words.

> **Answers**
> 1 window   2 wall   3 corner   4 radiator

2 Tell learners to read the text and label the furniture.

> **Answers**
> 1 cooker   2 table   3 sink   4 sofa   5 radiator
> 6 coffee table   7 TV   8 shower   9 bath
> 10 wardrobe   11 single bed   12 double bed

3 Ask learners to read the text and answer true or false.

> **Answers**
> 1 False   2 False   3 True   4 False   5 False

4 Go over the questions and practise them with correct stress and intonation. Put learners into pairs and tell them to ask each other the questions.

5 Tell learners to draw a plan of their home, including the furniture.

6 Tell learners to draw a square, then tell them where the furniture is in one of your rooms while they draw it. Then put learners in pairs and ask them to do the same using their plans from exercise 5.

Extension

Give learners some Post-it® notes and ask them to write the names of furniture on them. Tell them to stick them on the furniture in their rooms and learn them for next class.

Answers: Self-study exercises　　　　**A flat to rent**　　　　**Your own notes**

1 2 bedroom   3 living room   4 hall   5 bathroom

2 2 sofa   3 bath   4 radiator   5 wardrobe

3 2 next to   3 opposite   4 in the middle of

A flat to rent 7b

1 Label.

corner
door
radiator
wall
window

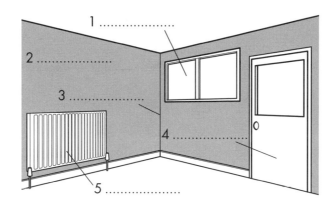

1 ....
2 ....
3 ....
4 ....
5 ....

2 Read and label the plan.

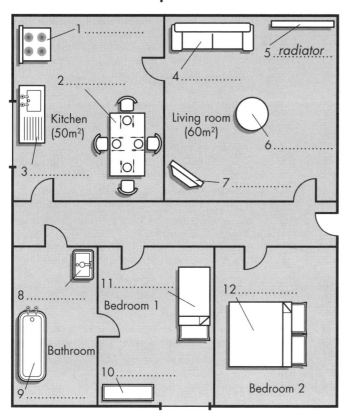

1 ....
2 ....
3 ....
4 ....
5 radiator
6 ....
7 ....
8 ....
9 ....
10 ....
11 ....
12 ....

Kitchen (50m²)

Living room (60m²)

Bedroom 1

Bathroom

Bedroom 2

For rent: modern flat with furniture

Description

On the right is the living room (60 m²). The living room has a radiator opposite the door and a TV in the corner. There is a coffee table in the middle of the room, and a sofa near the wall. The kitchen is 50 m². There are two doors to the kitchen. Under the kitchen window is a sink, with a cooker to the right of the sink. Next to the door are a table and chairs. The bathroom (20 m²) is opposite the kitchen. In the bathroom there is a bath and shower. Bedroom 1 (40 m²) has a single bed with a wardrobe next to the window. Bedroom 2 (45 m²) has a double bed.

3 Read again and write True or False.

1 The radiator is next to the door. ....
2 The coffee table is under the window. ....
3 The sink is to the right of the cooker. ....
4 The table and chairs are opposite the door. ....
5 The wardrobe is opposite the window. ....

4 Work together. Ask each other the questions.

In your house what is in your ...
1 living room?   2 kitchen?   3 bedroom?   4 bathroom?

5 Draw a plan of the rooms in your house, including your furniture.

6 Work in pairs. Student A, tell Student B about a room in your house. Student B, draw the room.

7c My room

Type of activity
Learners learn about things in a room and write a short description of their room.

AECC reference
Wt/E1.1, Ws/E1.1, Lr/E1.2a

Aims
Learners will practise composing a simple text to communicate basic information.

Language
describing your room; *next to, under, opposite, on the left/right of, on the back of*

Vocabulary
things, stuff, CDs, books, jewellery, pens, clothes, bag, on top of

Preparation
Photocopy the worksheet. Take in some items found in a person's room, e.g. jewellery, CDs, books and so on.

Differentiation
Weaker learners: ask them to make plurals from the other words in exercise 1.
Stronger learners: ask them to find and label the following in the picture in exercise 1: *computer, plant, poster, pillow, lamp, desk.*

Warmer

Play 'Hangman' with some of the vocabulary in exercise 1, e.g. *books, shelves, clothes.*

1 Ask learners what furniture they have in their room and what things they keep there. Tell learners to label the picture. Practise the pronunciation of the words. If you brought in any realia, you could pre-teach the vocabulary now.

> **Answers**
> 1 clothes 2 jewellery 3 books 4 shelves 5 CDs
> 6 quilt

2 Tell learners to look at the picture for one minute and try to remember what is in it. Then tell them to cover the picture and answer the questions.

> **Answers**
> 1 There are some shoes and a bag under the bed.
> 2 There are books and CDs on the shelves.
> 3 There is a quilt on the bed.
> 4 There are jewellery and pens on top of the cupboard.
> 5 There's a jacket on the back of the door.

3 Tell learners to look at the picture and complete the text.

4 (▶26) Play the recording and ask learners to check their answers to exercise 3.

> **Answers**
> 1 next 2 single 3 under 4 opposite 5 next
> 6 clothes 7 on the back

5 Tell learners to write the plural of the words.

> **Answers**
> 1 shelves 2 halves 3 scarves

6 Put learners in pairs and tell them to ask each other the questions.

7 Go over the table and ask them to write about their room.

Extension

Tell learners to write a text about their ideal room: how big a room they would like, what furniture they would like, what colour they would like it and what they would like in it.

Answers: Self-study exercises   **My room**   **Your own notes**

1 2 jewellery 3 scarf 4 CDs

2 2 under 3 on 4 in

My room 7c

1 Label the picture.

books
CDs
clothes
jewellery
quilt
shelves

3 ....
4 ....
5 ....
2 ....
1 ....
6 ....

2 Look at the picture for one minute. Cover the picture and answer the questions.

1 What is under the bed?
2 What are on the shelves?
3 What is on the bed?

4 What is on top of the cupboard?
5 What is on the back of the door?

3 Look at the picture and complete.

under   opposite   next (x2)   clothes   single   on the back

My room is very small. In my room I have a lot of stuff. My bed is (1) .... to the window. It's a (2) .... bed. I have a lot of things (3) .... the bed, like my bag and some shoes. I have two pillows and a quilt on my bed. There are some shelves (4) .... my bed with books and CDs on them. There is a cupboard (5) .... to the door. My cupboard is full of (6) .... , and I have my jewellery and pens on top of the cupboard. I keep my jacket and scarf (7) .... of the door. I'm not very tidy.

4 Listen and check.

5 Make plurals.

1 shelf ..... *shelves* .....   2 half ....   3 scarf ....

6 Work in pairs. Ask each other the questions.

1 What is in your room?   2 Are your tidy or untidy?

7 Write about your room.

My room is (very)	small. big.	In my room I (don't) have a lot of			things. stuff.
My	bed wardrobe shelves cupboard	is are	next to under opposite on the left/right of	the	window. door.
My	books CDs jewellery pens clothes bag	is are	on under in	my	shelves. cupboard. bed.
I'm a (very)	tidy untidy				person.

8a Sports, hobbies and interests

Type of activity
Learners listen to a conversation and then practise it. Individual and pair work.

AECC reference
Sc/E1.4a, Lr/E1.2b, Lr/E1.2e

Aims
Learners will practise making simple statements of fact.

Language
talking about ability; *can/can't; very well*

Vocabulary
cards, chess, backgammon, swimming, watching films, dancing, tennis, football, guitar, piano

Preparation
Photocopy the worksheet. Take in flashcards or photos of various sports, hobbies and interests.

Differentiation
Weaker learners: tell them to cover the words and write out the words for sports again with correct spelling. Stronger learners: ask them to add more games, interests and sports to the groups in exercise 2.

Warmer
Ask learners to work in groups and brainstorm for two minutes things people do in their spare time. The group with the most items is the winning group.

1 Ask learners to label the pictures. Practise the pronunciation of the words.

> **Answers**
> 1 playing cards   2 playing chess   3 swimming
> 4 playing the guitar   5 watching films   6 dancing
> 7 playing tennis   8 playing football
> 9 going shopping   10 playing backgammon

2 Tell learners to put the words into groups.

> **Answers**
> 1 playing cards, playing chess
> 2 playing tennis, playing football, swimming
> 3 playing the guitar, watching films, dancing, going shopping

3 (▶27) Tell learners to cover up the rest of the worksheet. Play the recording and tell learners to tick the words in exercise 1 they hear.

> **Answers**
> swimming ✓   playing cards ✓   dancing ✓
> playing the guitar ✓

4 (▶27) Play the recording again and tell learners to answer the questions.

> **Answers**
> 1 No
> 2 No
> 3 Yes – he's a great dancer.
> 4 The guitar

5 (▶27) Ask learners to listen again and tick the things people can do and cross the things people can't do.

> **Answers**
> Daniel ✓   Jessica ✗   Pranee ✗   Mia ✓   Ewa ✗

6 (▶28) Play the recording and practise the pronunciation of *can* and *can't*.

7 Tell learners to add three sports, interests or games to the table. Ask them to walk round the class asking questions and collecting information from the other learners.

Extension
Ask learners to write about the information they collected in exercise 7.

Answers: Self-study exercises	Sports, hobbies and interests	Your own notes

1 go: dancing, shopping
play: chess, football, tennis

2 2 can't   3 play   4 can   5 well

Sports, hobbies and interests 8a

1 Label the pictures

| dancing   going shopping   playing cards   playing chess   playing football |
| playing the guitar   playing tennis   swimming   watching films   playing backgammon |

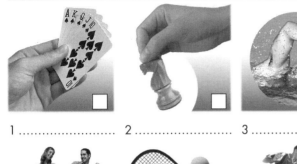

1 ....   2 ....   3 ....   4 ....   5 ....

6 ....   7 ....   8 ....   9 ....   10 ....

2 Put the words in exercise 1 into groups.

1 games: ...*playing cards*... , ... , ...
2 sports: .... , ... , ...
3 hobbies/interests: .... , ... , ... , ...

3 Listen and tick (✓) the things you hear in exercise 1.

4 Listen again and answer the questions. Write Yes or No.

1 Does Daniel want to go swimming? ....   3 Is Ben a good dancer? ....
2 Does Jessica play cards? ....   4 What instrument does Mia play? ....

5 Listen again and tick (✓) or cross (X).

	can (✓)	can't (X)
Daniel – swim		
Jessica – play cards		
Pranee – dance		
Mia – play the guitar		
Ewa – play the guitar		

6 Listen and practise.

✓ I can play the guitar.   I can dance very well.
X I can't swim.   I can't dance.

7 Work in pairs. Ask three other learners questions and complete the table.

Selma, can you play football?   Yes, I can. / No, I can't. / Yes, I can play very well.

game/sport/hobby	name	can	can't	can (very well)

8b Sports rules

Type of activity
Learners read a short text and decide which statements are true and which are false. Individual and group work.

AECC reference
Rt/E1.1a, Sc/E1.4a, Sc/E1.4d

Aims
Learners will practise following a short narrative on a familiar topic.

Language
can/can't; in front of, behind, in the middle of

Vocabulary
kick, head, score, save, catch, throw, hit

Preparation
Photocopy the worksheet. Take in flashcards or photos of sporting places/events such as Wimbledon, Ascot, Wembley, St Andrews.

Differentiation
Weaker learners: mime (or ask a learner to mime) some of the actions in exercise 2, e.g. *throw, catch, head*, and ask learners to say what the action is. Stronger learners: ask them to underline in the texts all the examples of things you can and can't do in the games in the texts.

Warmer

Ask learners which sports take place at these places – Wimbledon, Wembley, Ascot, St Andrews. If you brought in some pictures you could use these now.

1 Tell learners to match the words with the pictures.

> **Answers**
> 1 kick   2 head   3 save   4 score   5 catch
> 6 hit   7 throw

2 Ask learners to read the text and write True or False.

> **Answers**
> 1 False   2 False   3 True   4 False   5 True

3 Tell learners to read the texts again and tick or cross the sentences.

> **Answers**
> 1 ✓   2 ✓   3 ✗   4 ✗   5 ✗   6 ✓

4 Put learners into groups and tell them to ask each other the questions. Get feedback from one or two groups at the end of the activity.

Extension

Ask learners to find out about their local sports teams and which sports they can play in their area.

Answers: Self-study exercises   **Sports rules**   **Your own notes**

1 1 over   2 behind   3 in front of

2 2 kick   3 catch   4 score   5 throw   6 save

3 2 In a football game you can head the ball.
  3 In a football game you can't catch the ball.
  4 In a football game you can't kick another player.
  5 In a football game you can score a goal.

Sports rules 8b

1 Match the words with the pictures.

| catch | head | hit | kick | save | score | throw |

1 .... 2 .... 3 .... 4 ....

5 .... 6 .... 7 ....

2 Read and write True or False.

1 A game of rugby is ninety minutes long. ....
2 You can throw the ball in front of you in rugby. ....
3 Footballers can head the ball. ....
4 You can kick another player in a football game. ....
5 You get points in tennis when the other player can't hit the ball. ....

A rugby team has fifteen players and a match is eighty minutes. The field has two halves, with a goal in each half. You can score points by carrying the ball to the other end of the field. You can throw the ball, or kick the ball, but you can't throw the ball in front of you – only to a player behind you.

It's the world's favourite game! A football field has two halves, with a goal in each half. There are eleven players on each team and each team tries to score goals. In the game you can kick the ball or you can head the ball but you cannot touch the ball with your hands – only the goalkeeper can catch the ball and save it. You can kick the ball, but you can't kick another player!

Two or four people can play tennis. There is a net in the middle of the court and the players hit the ball over the net to each other. When one player can't hit the ball back, the other player wins a point.

3 Read the texts again and tick (✓) the things you can do. Cross (✗) the things you can't do.

In rugby you can …

1 carry the ball. ✓   2 throw the ball behind you. ☐

In football you can …

3 touch the ball with your hand. ☐   4 play with twelve people. ☐

In tennis …

5 five people can play. ☐   6 you can hit the ball over a net. ☐

4 Work in groups. Answer the questions.

1 Which famous sports people do you know?
2 Which British football teams do you know?
3 Which sports do people in your country play?

8c) Our sports centre

Type of activity
Learners write a short text about sports facilities.
Individual work.

AECC reference
Wt/E1.1, Ws/E1.1

Aims
Learners will practise writing simple sentences with correct word order and verb form.

Language
talking about ability; *good at; interested in; quite/very well*

Vocabulary
facilities at a sports centre: *pitch, crèche*; activities at a sports centre: *aerobics, yoga, table tennis, basketball, weight training*

Preparation
Photocopy the worksheet. Take in flashcards or photos of sports or things to do in a sports centre; brochures from sports centres.

Differentiation
Weaker learners: tell them to cover the words under the signs in exercise 1 and try to write the words again with correct spelling.
Stronger learners: ask them to look at the brochure and write one or two sentences about things you can or can't do at the sports centre.

Warmer

Ask learners to walk round and find someone who …
goes running, goes to the sports centre, goes swimming, plays football, does yoga. At the end of the activity get feedback.

1 Tell learners to write the names of the sports under the pictures.

> **Answers**
> 1 basketball   2 aerobics   3 table tennis   4 tennis
> 5 weight training   6 yoga

2 Ask learners to read the brochure and answer the questions.

> **Answers**
> 1 Yes, you can.
> 2 Yes, you can.
> 3 Yes, you can.
> 4 Yes, they can.
> 5 No, they can't.

3 Tell learners to read the application form and say which sports Hasan can do at the sports centre and which he can't.

> **Answers**
> He can play football and basketball. He can't do weight training.

4 Tell learners to complete the application form for themselves.

Extension

Ask learners to make a poster for their local sports centre or the college sports centre, or to find out what sports and activities are available there.

Answers: Self-study exercises   **Our sports centre**   **Your own notes**

1 2 table tennis   3 weight training   4 basketball
5 yoga

2 3 Ahmed can play football but he can't play tennis.
4 Mia can't swim but she can do aerobics.
5 Khaled can play table tennis and he can play basketball.
6 Latifa can't go running but she can do yoga.

Our sports centre 8c

1 Label the pictures.

| aerobics basketball table tennis tennis weight training yoga |

1 .... 2 .... 3 .... 4 .... 5 .... 6 ....

2 Read and answer.

1 Can you play football at the sports centre? *Yes, you can.* ....

2 Can you go swimming there?
....

3 Can you get a cup of coffee there?
....

4 Can someone take care of your children at the sports centre?
....

5 Can children play basketball?
....

═══ Green Lane Sports Centre ═══

Opening hours: Monday to Saturday 9 am–10 pm
Sunday 10 am–6 pm

Facilities: 5-a-side football pitches (x3); basketball court; swimming pool; crèche (6 weeks to 2 years old); café

Classes		Adult	Junior
Keep fit:	aerobics	✓	✓
	yoga	✓	✗
Sports:	table tennis	✓	✓
	5-a-side football	✓	✓
	basketball	✓	✗
	swimming	✓	✓

3 Read the application form. Write about the sports Hasan can or can't do at the sports centre.

He can play football.

═══ Green Lane Sports Centre Application form ═══

Name: Hasan Sharif   Address: 56 Graham Road

Tel: 0207 219 6538   Postcode: E8 1BP

Which sports are you interested in? How well can you play?

I would like to play 5-a-side football. I'm quite good at football. I'm also interested in weight training and basketball. I can play basketball very well, but I'm not good at weight training — is there a trainer for this?

4 Complete the application form.

═══ Green Lane Sports Centre Application form ═══

Name: ....   Address: ....

Tel: ....   Postcode: ....

Which sports are you interested in? How well can you play?

I	would like want	to play	5-a-side football. basketball. tennis. table tennis.	I can	play	5-a-side football basketball tennis table tennis	very well. well. quite well.
		to do	yoga. aerobics. weight training.		do	yoga aerobics weight training	

I'm (not) good at	5-a-side football. basketball. table tennis. yoga. aerobics. weight training.
I'm (not) interested in	

A single to Oxford Street

Type of activity
Learners listen to a conversation and then practise it. Individual and pair work.

AECC reference
Sc/E1.2a, Sc/E1.3b, Lr E1.2e

Aims
Learners will practise making requests for things or actions and asking for information.

Language
making requests; present continuous affirmative

Vocabulary
single, return, Travelcard

Preparation
Photocopy the worksheet. Take in single, return and day saver (or the equivalent) bus tickets.

Differentiation
Weaker learners: photocopy one of the conversations from the audioscript and turn it into a gap fill. Play the recording again for learners to complete.
Stronger learners: choose a conversation and play it again line by line, stopping after each line for learners to write it down until they have the complete conversation.

Warmer
Ask learners to walk round and ask each other how they come to college – find out how many walk, and how many come by bus or by car. At the end of five minutes, get feedback from the class.

1 Go over the signs and ask them to match the signs with the phrases.

> **Answers**
> a 4   b 3   c 2   d 1

2 Go over the tickets and ask learners to label the tickets with the words. Practise the pronunciation of the words.

> **Answers**
> 1 single   2 return   3 Travelcard

3 (▶29) Tell learners to listen and circle the tickets the people ask for or have.

> **Answers**
> 1 return   2 single   3 Travelcard

4 (▶29) Tell learners to cover up exercises 5 and 6. Play the recording again and tell learners to write true or false.

> **Answers**
> 1 False   2 True   3 True   4 False   5 True

5 (▶30) Play the recording and tell learners to listen and practise.

6 Put learners into pairs and ask them to complete the conversation.

> **Answers**
> 1 'd like   2 are you   3 single   4 please
> 5 Thank you

7 Put learners into pairs and tell them to practise the conversation with local places and streets.

Extension
Ask learners to look for more signs on buses, and to remember or draw them for the next class.

Answers: Self-study exercises   **A single to Oxford Street**   **Your own notes**

1 1 Travelcard   2 single   3 return
2 2 Where   3 single   4 return   5 That's

A single to Oxford Street (9a)

1 Match the sentences with the signs.

a Listen to music quietly.
b Push the bell to stop the bus.
c Pay with the correct money.
d Pay the driver for the ticket.

1 .... 2 .... 3 .... 4 ....

Please pay driver

EXACT CHANGE ONLY

Press bell to stop

Use headphones with consideration

2 Match.

1 one journey   a

Bus Ticket SINGLE

2 a journey to a place and back again   b

TRAVEL CARD
ALL DAY TRAVEL ON ANY BUS

3 all day travel on any bus or train   c

Train Ticket
RETURN

3 Listen and circle the ticket they buy or have.

1 return / single / Travelcard   2 return / single / Travelcard   3 return / single / Travelcard

4 Listen again and write True or False.

conversation 1 A return ticket is £5.   1 ....
conversation 2 One of the passengers asks the driver where the bus goes.   2 ....
conversation 2 The passengers want to go to college.   3 ....
conversation 3 The passengers are going to three places.   4 ....
conversation 3 The passengers don't know when to get off the bus.   5 ....

5 Listen and practise.

I'd like a ticket to the city centre, please.   *Hi, we're going to Hyde Park.*
Two tickets to South Thames College, please.   *Can you tell us when to get off?*

6 Work together. Complete the conversation.

| are you   please   single   thank you   'd like |

Passenger: I (1) .... a ticket to the city centre, please.
Bus driver: Where (2) .... going?
Passenger: Oxford Street.
Bus driver: Is that a (3) .... or return?
Passenger: Return, please.
Bus driver: That's four pounds, (4) ....
Passenger: (5) ....

7 Work together. Practise the conversation using places in your area.

9b Travel pass

Type of activity
Learners read a brochure about travel pass types and match descriptions with type of pass. Individual and pair work.

AECC reference
Rt/E1.1b, Rt/E1.2, Sc/E1.4a

Aims
Learners will practise obtaining information from texts.

Language
asking for information; *any + thing/where/time/one*

Vocabulary
senior, pass, permit, standard

Preparation
Photocopy the worksheet. Take in different bus/train/travel passes or brochures for these, and different travel tickets: train, bus, child ticket.

Differentiation
Weaker learners: ask one or two more questions about each text, e.g.
text 1: What time can people over 60 travel for free?
text 2: For people with a free school pass, how far is the school from their home?
text 3: What do young people need to get a bus saver pass?
Stronger learners: ask them to write a few sentences about when they use, and why they have, a travel pass.

Warmer
Play 'Hangman' with words from the text: *pass, fare, saver, permit*. If you have brought in any tickets or passes, use them to pre-teach some vocabulary.

1 Tell learners to read the texts quickly and find the answers.

> **Answers**
> 1 Free school travel pass
> 2 Bus Saver
> 3 Senior permit

2 Ask learners to read the texts again and decide which pass is good for which person.

> **Answers**
> 1 Free school travel pass
> 2 Senior permit
> 3 Bus Saver

3 Ask learners to read the text again and complete the words beginning with *any*. Explain that we use *any* when it is not important to say which thing we are talking about.

> **Answers**
> 1 anyone   2 any time   3 anywhere   4 anything

4 Tell learners to complete the sentences with *anyone, any time, anywhere* or *anything*.

> **Answers**
> 1 anywhere   2 anyone   3 any time

5 Tell learners to work in pairs and ask each other the questions. At the end of the activity get feedback from one or two pairs.

Extension
Tell learners to find out what travel passes are available in their town or city. Ask them to go to the train station and get leaflets on three different types of passes or tickets.

Answers: Self-study exercises | Travel pass | **Your own notes**

1 2 anywhere   3 anything   4 anyone
2 2 £20   3 a year

Travel pass (9b)

1 Read and answer.

Which pass is for people over …
1 six years old? .... 2 sixteen years old? .... 3 sixty years old? ....

City travel passes

Senior permit
Anyone over 60 can travel for free on buses and trains, any time between 9.30 am and 12 pm Monday to Friday, and all day at weekends. Before 9.30 am, you pay the standard fare.

Free school travel pass
You can have a free bus to school when it is over two miles from your home to school and when your child is under ten.

Bus Saver
For young people just starting work, or for students in full-time education. You can use this on any bus, anywhere, any time. People between 16 and 21 need a photo and anything with your age on it.

---

2 Read again and match the people with the passes.

Li Li

My daughter is seven. We go to school together, but it is over an hour to walk there – it's very far.

Samira

In the week I get the bus to town. On Saturday and Sunday I like to visit my family and I catch the bus or walk. I'm 65 and I like to see my grandchildren.

Monika

I study at City College, and my classes start at ten o'clock in the morning. I don't have a lot of money and I want to use my pass to go to different places.

1 .... 2 .... 3 ....

3 Read the text in exercise 2 again. Complete the words beginning with *any*.

1 any........*one*........
2 any ....
3 any ....
4 any ....

4 Complete the sentences with answers from exercise 4.

I can't find my bus pass (1) .... Does (2) .... know where I put it?
When do you want to meet – morning or afternoon? It doesn't matter – (3) ....

5 Work together. Ask each other the questions.

1 How do you come to class?
2 Do you have a travel pass?
3 What do you need for your travel pass?

9c Travelling

Type of activity
Learners write about their preferences, and walk round and do a learner survey. Individual and class work.

AECC reference
Ws/E1.1, Wt/E1.1

Aims
Learners will practise composing a simple text to communicate ideas, with correct basic word order and verb form.

Language
expressing likes and preferences; *like + -ing* form

Vocabulary
bus, car, taxi, train, tram; comfortable, quick, slow, relaxing, crowded, cheap, expensive

Preparation
Photocopy the worksheet. Take in flashcards of different forms of transport.

Differentiation
Weaker learners: write on the board *love, like, don't like, hate*. Revise different forms of transport and ask learners to draw a table:

name			
plane			
train			
taxi			

Tell them to go round the class and collect information from other learners about how they prefer to travel. Stronger learners: ask them to write a few sentences about the transport system in the town or city where they live and what they think about it.

Warmer
Ask learners to work in groups and think of as many forms of transport as they can. If you brought flashcards in, you could use them to pre-teach the vocabulary.

1 Tell them to match the words with the pictures and practise the pronunciation of the words.

> **Answers**
> 1 bus 2 tram 3 train 4 car 5 taxi

2 Ask learners which form of transport is comfortable, quick, slow, relaxing or crowded.

3 Tell learners to read the texts and complete the table.

> **Answers**
>
> | | Which is your favourite way of travelling? | Why? |
> |--|--|------|
> | Kim | tram | relaxing |
> | Constancia | taxi | easy to go back home |
> | Ahmed | car | comfortable and quick |

4 Tell learners to walk round the class and ask other learners how they prefer to travel and why.

5 Ask learners to write a short paragraph about how they prefer to travel and why.

Extension
Ask learners to write a few sentences about the other learners in their class, using the information from exercise 4.

Answers: Self-study exercises — Travelling — Your own notes

1 2 comfortable/quick/cheap
   3 comfortable/quick/cheap
   4 cheap

2 1 like/prefer
   2 easy/quick/cheap
   3 favourite
   4 is by
   5 quick/relaxing/comfortable

Travelling 9c

1 Label the pictures.

| bus | car | taxi | train | tram |

1 .... 2 .... 3 .... 4 .... 5 ....

2 Say which is ...

1 comfortable   2 quick   3 slow   4 relaxing   5 crowded.

3 Read and complete.

	Which is your favourite way of travelling?	Why?
Kim		
Constancia		
Ahmed		

Kim
I live in the city centre, so the shops are near to my house. I take the bus, but taxis are too expensive. Sometimes I walk home. My favourite way of travelling is the tram. It's very relaxing.

Constancia
My children go to a school two kilometres away. I go by bus to meet them because it's cheap. I prefer taking a taxi to the town centre – it's easy to go home with my shopping bags. I don't travel by train – I don't go very far from my home!

Ahmed
I like driving, so I travel by car a lot. Cars are my favourite way of travelling. When I travel to another city, I prefer going by car because it's comfortable and quick.

4 Ask the other students the questions in exercise 3.

5 Write about yourself.

I	like prefer	travelling	by	car train tram bus taxi	because it's	comfortable. quick. easy. relaxing. cheap.
My favourite way of travelling is						

I don't like travelling by		car train tram bus taxi	because it's	expensive. slow. crowded.

10a Can you tell me the way to the bus station?

Type of activity
Learners listen to conversations and then practise asking for directions. Individual and pair work.

AECC reference
Sc/E1.3b, Sc/E1.3c, Lr/E1.3b

Aims
Learners will practise listening and asking for information, listening and asking for directions and location, and making statements of fact.

Language
asking for directions; prepositions of direction

Vocabulary
traffic lights, bus stop, bus station, zebra crossing, car park

Preparation
Photocopy the worksheet and if possible photocopy the map onto an OHT. Take in maps of the learners' town or city.

Differentiation
Weaker learners: ask them to write a similar conversation to the one in exercise 5, using places in their town or city.
Stronger learners: ask them what other road and street signs they have seen and if they know the meaning of these.

Warmer
Put learners into groups and ask them to look at the map and find: the town hall, a church, a cinema, a bank and a school. Give one point to the group which finds each place first. The group with the most answers is the winner.

1 Tell learners to match the instructions with the road signs.

> **Answers**
> 1 turn left   2 turn right   3 go straight on

2 Tell learners to label the map with the words and then practise the pronunciation of the words with them.

> **Answers**
> 1 zebra crossing   2 traffic lights   3 car park
> 4 bus stop   5 bus station

3 (▶31) Tell learners to cover up exercises 4 and 5. Play the recording and tell learners to draw the routes as they listen. If you have copied the map onto an OHT, you could use it now to show learners how to do the exercise.

> **Answers**
>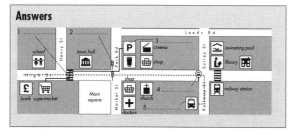

4 (▶32) Play the recording and tell learners to listen and practise the ways of asking for directions.

5 (▶31) Play the recording from exercise 3 again. Learners listen and complete the conversations.

> **Answers**
> 1 tell   2 Go down   3 Turn right   4 on your right
> 5 how can   6 left   7 traffic lights   8 go straight
> 9 Go across

6 Put learners in pairs and tell them to ask each other for directions using the map in exercise 2 or using maps of their town or city.

Extension
Ask learners to look for more shops, places and things in the street and get ready to tell the other learners the names of these things for the next class.

Answers: Self-study exercises   Can you tell me the way to the bus station?   **Your own notes**

1 2 car park   3 zebra crossing   4   traffic lights

2 1 turn right   2 turn left   3 go straight on

3 2 turn/go   3 straight   4 your/the

Can you tell me the way to the bus station? 10a

1 Match the words with the signs.

| go straight on |
| turn left |
| turn right |

1 .... 2 .... 3 ....

2 Label the map.

| bus station   bus stop   car park   traffic lights   zebra crossing |

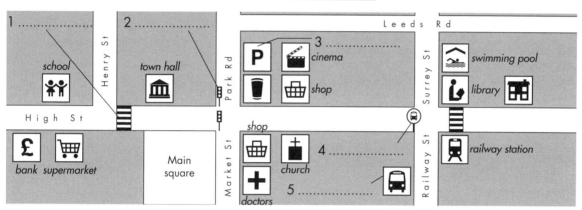

L e e d s   R d

1 ....
2 ....
3 .... cinema
swimming pool
school
town hall
shop
library
High St
shop
railway station
£ bank supermarket
Main square
church
4 ....
5 ....
doctors
Henry St
Park Rd
Market St
Surrey St
Railway St

3 Listen to the conversations and draw the routes.

4 Listen and practise.

Can you tell me the way to the bus station?   *How can I get to the supermarket?*

5 Listen again and complete the conversations.

1   Sergei: Excuse me, can you (1) .... me the way to the bus station?
   Man: OK, we are here, at the school.
   Sergei: Yes.
   Man: (2) .... the High Street.
   Sergei: OK.
   Man: Go across Market Street and Park Road.
   Sergei: Yes.
   Man: (3) .... at the bus stop and go down Railway Street.
   Sergei: OK.
   Man: The bus station is (4) .... , on Railway Street.
   Sergei: Thank you.

| on your right |
| left |
| go across |
| go down |
| how can |
| tell |
| turn right |
| go straight |
| traffic lights |

2   Nongluck: Excuse me, (5) .... I get to the supermarket?
   Woman: From the car park, turn (6) .... and go down Park Road.
   Nongluck: OK.
   Woman: When you get to the (7) .... , turn right.
   Nongluck: Yes.
   Woman: Then (8) .... on.
   Nongluck: I see.
   Woman: (9) .... the road at the zebra crossing, and the supermarket is opposite the school.
   Nongluck: Thank you very much.

6 Work together. Student A, ask Student B for directions from the supermarket to the swimming pool. Student B, ask Student A for directions from the bus station to the doctor's.

10b Visitors' day

Type of activity
Learners read a brochure and transfer information.
Individual work.

AECC reference
Rs/E1.1a, Rt/E1.1b

Aims
Learners will practise reading to obtain information from texts.

Language
saying how far somewhere is; *How long does it take from ... to ... ?, How far is ... ?, How many kilometres is ... ?*

Vocabulary
programme, tour, theatre, hill, metre, kilometre

Preparation
Photocopy the worksheet. Take in a visitors' day brochure from your college.

Differentiation
Weaker learners: dictate some of the words from the text to them like *programme, museum, theatre* and *college*.
Stronger learners: ask them to write two or three more sentences following exercise 4 about distances on the map.

Warmer

Ask learners how people in Britain usually measure distance – inches, feet, yards, miles – and how many kilometres equals one mile (one mile = just over 1.6 kilometres).

1 Tell learners to read the brochure and answer the questions.

> **Answers**
> 1 Visitors' day   2 15 minutes   3 50 metres
> 4 one kilometre

2 Tell learners to read the text again and complete the routes on the map.

Answers

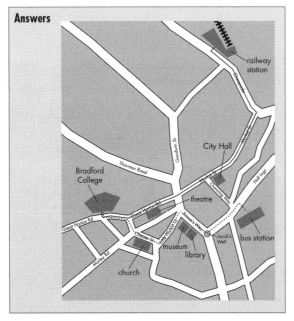

3 Put learners into pairs and tell them to ask each other questions about the distance to places in their town or city.

Extension

Ask learners to work in groups and produce a poster for a visitors' day to your college, school, department or class.

Answers: Self-study exercises　　　　**Visitors' day**　　　　**Your own notes**

1 2 How long does it take to get to the college?
　　3 How many metres is it to the bus stop?

2 D

Visitors' day (10b)

1 Read and answer the questions.

1 What is happening on 7th April? ....
2 How long does it take to walk to the college from the railway station? ....
3 How far is the theatre from the college? ....
4 How many kilometres is the college from the bus station? ....

**Bradford College
Richmond Road
Bradford BD7**

Visitors' day
Date: 7th April
Time: 10 am—3 pm

Programme
Welcome from Head of College
Tour of college
Tea
Questions

Directions to college

It takes 15 minutes to walk from Forster Square railway station to the college. When you come out of the railway station, turn left. Go down the hill and turn right down Market Street. Go past the City Hall and walk past the theatre. Go up the hill on Great Horton Road. After about 50 metres, the college is on your right.

From the bus station the college is about one kilometre. Go past Jacob's Well to the library. Go past the museum and turn left. Go up Little Horton Lane and turn right at Chester Street. Go past the church. At the end of Chester Street, turn left and go up Great Horton Road. The college is on your right.

2 Read again and draw the routes to the college on the map from ...

1 the railway station
2 the bus station.

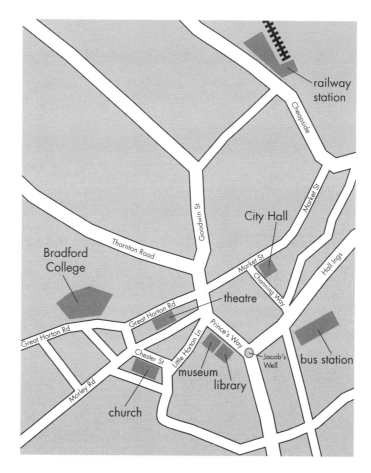

3 Work together. Ask each other questions about places in your town or city.

How far is the railway station from the college?   *It's about 500 metres.*

10c Where's the party?

Type of activity
Learners write letters of invitation and give directions. Individual work.

AECC reference
Wt/E1.1, Ws/E1.1

Aims
Learners will practise writing a simple text to communicate basic information and construct simple sentences.

Language
giving directions; *until* for distances; *(go) past*; ordinal numbers below ten

Vocabulary
party, driving test, celebrate, end of term

Preparation
Photocopy the worksheet. Take in some invitation cards.

Differentiation
Weaker learners: photocopy one of the letters with some words blanked out and dictate it back for them to fill it in. Stronger learners: give them a point on the map and ask them to write directions to another place on the map, e.g. from Suffolk Street to the railway station.

Warmer
Ask learners who likes parties and what kind of parties they can think of – birthday parties, leaving parties, end of term parties, welcome parties and so on.

1 Tell learners to read the letters and answer the questions.

> **Answers**
> 1 A   2 C   3 B   4 D

2 Tell learners to read the letters again and find where the parties are on the map. If you wish, you could put learners in groups and do this as a competition.

Answers

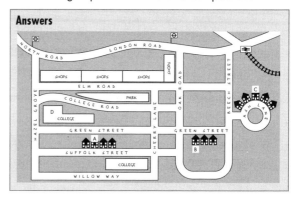

3 Tell learners to use the writing frame and write an invitation with dates and directions to where the party will take place.

Extension
Tell learners to give their invitation to another learner and then reply to the invitation.

Answers: Self-study exercises

Where's the party?

Your own notes

1 1 Road   2 Street   3 Lane
2 2 celebrate   3 party   4 at

Where's the party? (10c)

1 Read the letters and answer the questions.

Which party is for …

1 a birthday? ....
2 a new house? ....
3 a driving test? ....
4 the end of classes? ....

A

10 Today!

My son Faustin is ten today. Please come to his birthday party on Monday at 12.
Jemal

Directions:
Turn left out of the train station and walk down London Road until you get to Oak Road. Go past the shops and take the fourth street on the right. Our house is the third on the right on Suffolk Street.

B

New driver!

I passed my driving test – come and help us celebrate. The party is on Saturday at 4.
Maryam

Directions:
Get off the bus at North Road and walk down Hazel Grove. Go past Elm Road and take the next turn down College Rd. When you get to Cherry Lane, turn right and take the next left into Green Street. We live in the first house on the right.

C

New Home!

We have got a new house.
Come and look.
Wei

Directions

Take the bus to London Road and walk down Oak Road. Take the first left down Elm Road and go right at Beech Street. At Ash Lane, turn left and turn left again. Our house is the third on the left.

D

End of term party

It's our last day of classes. Come and celebrate with us from 6 – 8 on Friday evening.
Fatima

Directions
By train: turn left and go down London Road. Take the first left down Beech Street then turn right down Elm Road until you come to Cherry Lane. Turn left down Cherry Lane until you get to College Road. Turn right into College Road and Park College is on your left.

2 Read the letters again and find the parties on the map.

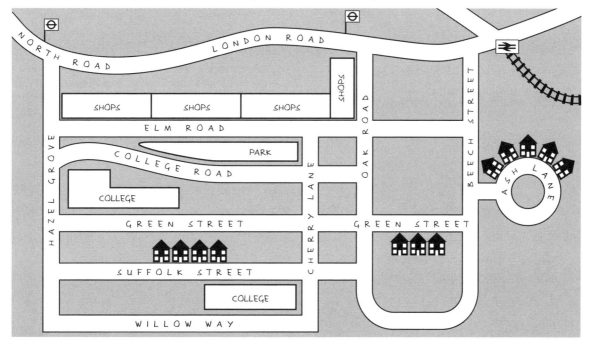

3 Write an invitation letter.

Test success!

We are having a party. Party time!	Come and celebrate with us. Please come to our party. Come and help us celebrate.	(date/day/time)	(place)	(directions)

11a What's my job?

Type of activity
Learners listen to a quiz game and then practise asking questions. Individual and group work.

AECC reference
Sc/E1.4d, Lr/E1.1c, Lr/E1.4b

Aims
Learners will practise giving a description and asking for information.

Language
asking for information; present simple *yes/no* questions and short answers

Vocabulary
taxi driver, nurse, secretary, builder, cleaner, teacher, shop assistant, cook

Preparation
Make two sets of photocopies. Cut out the cards from exercise 6 from one set. Take in flashcards of different jobs.

Differentiation
Weaker learners: tell them to ask you 20 questions and try to guess the job you are thinking of.
Stronger learners: ask them to write more questions for exercise 5 to ask during the group work.

Warmer

Put learners into groups and tell them to think of as many jobs as they can in three minutes. If you have brought in flashcards of jobs, you could use these now to pre-teach more jobs.

1 Tell learners to label the pictures with the words. Practise the pronunciation of the words.

> **Answers**
> 1 taxi driver   2 nurse   3 secretary   4 builder
> 5 cleaner

2 Ask learners to read the sentences and match them with the jobs.

> **Answers**
> 1 secretary   2 cleaner   3 builder   4 nurse
> 5 taxi driver

3 (▶33) Tell learners they will listen to a quiz. As they listen they should try to guess the job. NOTE: there is a pause in the recording for learners to give their answers.

> **Answers**
> 1 nurse   2 builder

4 (▶34) Play the recording and ask learners to practise the *yes/no* questions and short answers.

5 Ask learners to write out the questions in full.

> **Answers**
> 1 Do you work inside/outside?
> 2 Do you work full-time/part-time?
> 3 Do you work alone/with people?
> 4 Do you work with machines/computers/your hands?
> 5 Do you work in a shop/an office/a kitchen?

6 Put learners into groups. Give out the cards. Tell them to ask *yes/no* questions to guess the job. Remind learners that they only have 20 questions to get the right answer.

Extension

Ask learners to write down the jobs of five people they meet and report back to the class in the next lesson.

Answers: Self-study exercises   **What's my job?**   **Your own notes**

1 1 D   2 C   3 B   4 A

2 2 Do you work with people or machines?
3 Do you work in a big place?
4 Do you work in a factory?

What's my job? 11a

1 Label the pictures.

builder   cleaner   nurse   secretary   taxi driver

1 ....   2 ....   3 ....   4 ....   5 ....

2 Match the sentences with the jobs.

1 I type letters and answer telephones in an office.   .... *secretary* ....
2 I clean and tidy rooms and offices.   ....
3 I build buildings.   ....
4 I look after people in hospital.   ....
5 I drive people to places.   ....

3 Listen to a quiz and guess the jobs.

4 Listen and practise the questions and answers.

Do you work in a hospital?	*Yes, I do.*
Do you work in a factory?	*No, I don't.*
Do you get a lot of money?	*No, not really.*
Do you like your job?	*Yes, I do.*
Do you work with your hands?	*Yes and no.*

5 Write questions.

Example *Do you work inside?*

1 work inside/outside   ....
2 work full-time/part-time   ....
3 work alone/with people   ....
4 work with machines/computers/your hands   ....
5 work in a shop/office/kitchen   ....

6 Work in groups. One learner takes a card. The other learners ask questions to guess the job.

Secretary	**Shop assistant**
work in an office	take and give money
answer telephone	serve people
write letters	tidy up
give messages	put things out
Teacher	**Cook**
prepare classes	prepare food
mark homework	cook food
go to meetings	plan menus
help students	wash pans

11b Person wanted

Type of activity
Learners read job advertisements and match people with the jobs. Individual and pair work.

AECC reference
Rs/E1.1a, Rt/E1.1b

Aims
Learners will practise reading and obtaining information from a text.

Language
understanding abbreviations; *needed, wanted*

Vocabulary
nursery, chef, busy, information technology, per hour

Preparation
Photocopy the worksheet. Take in more job advertisements from a local newspaper.

Differentiation
Weaker learners: ask them to think of more jobs and write them out.
Stronger learners: ask them to write an advert for a job using some of the abbreviations.

Warmer

Put learners into groups. Tell them that for each job they spell correctly they will get one point. Say five jobs (e.g. *chef, assistant, secretary, builder, cleaner*). The group with the most correctly spelled jobs is the winner.

1 Ask learners where they can find job adverts like these. Tell them to match the pictures with the adverts.

Answers
1 B cleaner   2 D chef   3 A shop assistant
4 C office assistant

2 Ask learners to read the advertisements again and find the abbreviations of the words. If you have brought in a local newspaper, you could ask learners to look through it and find more examples of the abbreviations.

Answers
1 Tel   2 ph   3 hrs   4 P/T   5 K   6 IT   7 Mon
8 pm

3 Tell learners to read the advertisements and answer the questions.

Answers
1 two
2 chef
3 after six o'clock in the evening
4 11–13 thousand pounds a year

4 Tell learners to read about the people and decide which job is good for them.

Answers
Jean – shop assistant
Atakan – office assistant

5 Put learners in groups of four and ask them to decide on a job for each learner in the group.

Extension

Ask learners to write a list of what is needed to be a manager or a good learner.

Answers: Self-study exercises   **Person wanted**   **Your own notes**

1 2 part-time
3 information technology
4 Monday
5 thousand

2 2 want
3 want
4 need

3 2 part-time
3 two
4 Thursday to Saturday

Person wanted (11b)

1 Read and match the adverts with the pictures.

1 ....   2 ....   3 ....   4 ....

A
Busy sandwich bar in Ashton
Shop assistant needed
Mon–Fri
9 am–3 pm
Tel 0161 304 0061 after 6 pm

B
Tots Nursery
P/T cleaner wanted for
children's nursery school.
2 hrs 9 – 11 am.
Mon – Sun, £5.50 ph.
Phone Nicola Tel: 0161 333 9740

C
Office assistant
Person wanted for busy office
Good IT skills
£11K to £13K
City centre
0845 838 7814

D
Chef needed for cafe.
About 20 hours
Mon – Fri.
Good pay.
Tel Mark 07796 6673145.

2 Find the abbreviations of these words in the advertisements.

1 telephone number ....*Tel*........
2 per hour ....
3 hours ....
4 part-time ....
5 thousand ....
6 information technology ....
7 Monday ....
8 afternoon/evening ....

3 Read again and answer.

1 How many hours a day does the cleaner work? ....
2 What is another word for a *cook*? ....
3 When can you call about the shop assistant job? ....
4 How much money does the office assistant earn? ....

4 Read and match the people with the jobs in exercise 1.

I'm Jean. I have two children and I take them to school in the morning and bring them home in the afternoon. I can only work after 8.30 until 4.00. I don't want to do too much work and I don't need a lot of money.

My name's Atakan and I'm from Turkey. I want a full-time job that has good pay. I like working with people and I'm good at working with computers. I'd like to work in the city centre too.

5 Work in groups. Decide on a job for the learners in your group.

Example: *Latifa can work in a café – she's a good cook.*

11c) A job application

Type of activity
Learners write a letter of application for a job. Individual, pair and group work.

AECC reference
Wt/E1.1, Ws/E1.3, Sc/E1.1b

Aims
Learners will practise writing a simple text to communicate basic ideas and using basic punctuation to write about oneself.

Language
describing your character; *would like*

Vocabulary
hard-working, lazy, polite, rude, disorganised, organised, available, apply

Preparation
Photocopy the worksheet.

Differentiation
Weaker learners: ask them to cover the words in exercise 1 and try to write them again with correct spelling. Stronger learners: ask them to write a job advert using some of the abbreviations in Unit 11b (if you have done this previously) and words from 11c.

Warmer
Play 'Hangman' with one or two of the adjectives in exercise 1.

1 Ask learners to match the words with the pictures.

> **Answers**
> 1 lazy   2 organised   3 polite

2 Ask learners to write the opposites.

> **Answers**
> hard-working – lazy
> rude – polite
> disorganised – organised

3 Tell learners to read the advertisement and complete the letter.

> **Answers**
> 1 Mr   2 apply   3 shop   4 polite   5 hard-working
> 6 available   7 Yours sincerely

4 Put learners into pairs, with Student A completing the advert and Student B writing a letter for the advert. Tell Student A to add more information to the advert, e.g. name, address and so on.

5 Ask learners to read the letters and adverts from the other learners and think of questions a person might ask at an interview.

6 Tell the Student A to interview Student B for the job.

Extension
Give learners an appropriate job advert from the local paper and ask them write a short letter for it.

Answers: Self-study exercises

A job application

Your own notes

1 1 A   2 D   3 B   4 C

2 2 Learners' own answers
3 Learners' own answers
4 available
5 evening/afternoon/morning
6 Yours sincerely

A job application (11c)

1 Match the words with the people in the picture.

| lazy   organised   polite |

2 Write the opposites for the words in 1.

| disorganised   hard-working   rude |

3 Read the advertisement and complete the letter.

| apply   available   hard-working   Mr   polite   shop   yours sincerely |

Shop assistant

£150 per week

Mon – Fri 8 am – 5 pm

Person wanted for shop work: selling and unpacking goods. Must be polite and hard-working and available to work at weekends.

Apply to: Tom Williamson Grocer's, High Street, Newtown, NW4

Dear (1) .... Williamson,

I would like to (2) .... for the job of assistant in your (3) .... I am (4) .... and (5) .... and I am (6) .... for work all week.

(7) .... ,

(your name) ....

4 Work together. Student A, complete the advert. Student B, write a letter for the job.

Student A

School assistant needed

£ .... per hour, ... hrs a week – .... and .... person needed to work in local school. Must be available .... – ....

Student B

Dear Sir / Madam,

| I am writing about the | job of position of | ... | in your | shop. factory. restaurant. ... |

| | I am | hard-working organised polite | and |

| hard-working. organised. polite. | I can | am available for | work | in the at the | morning. evening. afternoon. weekend. |

Yours sincerely,
(Name)

**5 Student B, read Student A's advert and think of questions to ask about it.
Student A, read Student B's letter and think of questions to ask.**

6 Student A, interview Student B for the job.

12a Would you like a drink?

Type of activity
Learners listen to conversations and then practise making offers and requests. Individual and group work.

AECC reference
Sc/E1.4d, Lr/E1.2e, Sd/E1.1c

Aims
Learners will practise listening to and making offers and requests.

Language
making offers and requests; talking about likes and dislikes; *Would you like ... ?, Could I ... ?, Can I ... ?*

Vocabulary
crisps, chocolate, biscuit, white/black, tea/coffee, cola, sandwich, milk, water, orange juice

Preparation
Photocopy the worksheet. Take in different snacks and drinks. Make a copy of the audioscript for conversation 2.

Differentiation
Weaker learners: write some of the questions from exercise 6 on the board with the words in the wrong order and tell them to write the questions again with correct word order.
Stronger learners: ask them to read the conversation and underline more ways of making offers and requests.

Warmer
Ask learners what their favourite drinks are and what they drink during the day normally. If you have brought in some snacks and drinks, you could pre-teach the vocabulary with these now.

1 Tell learners to complete the mind map with the words in the box. Practise the pronunciation of the words.

> **Answers**
> 1 tea   2 coffee   3 cake   4 biscuits   5 milk
> 6 water   7 sandwich   8 crisps

2 (▶35) Tell learners to cover up exercise 4. Then ask learners to listen to the conversations and choose the correct answer.

> **Answers**
> 1 a   2 b

3 (▶35) Tell learners to listen again and tick the things they hear in exercise 1.

> **Answers**
> drink ✓   water ✓   tea ✓   biscuit ✓   coffee ✓
> cake ✓

4 Ask learners to complete the conversations with the phrases and sentences in the boxes.

5 (▶35) Play the recording as learners listen and check their answers.

> **Answers**
> 1 Could I have
> 2 Would you like
> 3 What can I get you?
> 4 can I get
> 5 can I get you
> 6 for you

6 (▶36) Play the recording and ask learners to practise the questions.

7 Put learners into pairs and ask them to practise one of the conversations. Tell them to choose other items from exercise 1, if they like.

Extension
Ask learners to write another conversation using offers and requests.

Answers: Self-study exercises | **Would you like a drink?** | **Your own notes**

1 2 A cup of coffee with milk and one spoon of sugar.
  3 A cup of tea with no milk and two spoons of sugar.

2 1 don't like   2 like   3 love

3 1 asking for something:
  Can I have a biscuit?, Can I get a coffee?
  2 offering something:
  Can I get you anything?, Would you like something to eat?, What can I get you?

Would you like a drink? 12a

1 Complete.

biscuits
cake
coffee
~~cola~~
crisps
milk
sandwich
tea
water

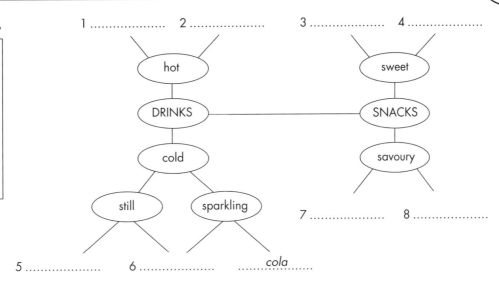

1 .... 2 .... 3 .... 4 ....

hot

DRINKS ——————— SNACKS

sweet

cold

savoury

still   sparkling

7 .... 8 ....

5 ....   6 .... *cola* ......

2 Listen and choose a or b.

| conversation 1 | The people are | (a) in someone's house. | (b) in a café. |
| conversation 2 | The people are | (a) in a restaurant. | (b) at a coffee bar. |

3 Listen again and tick (✓) the things you hear in exercise 1.

4 Complete the conversations.

Could I have   What can I get you?   Would you like

1   Jessica: Hi, Jolanta. Hello, Nongluck. Come in.
  Nongluck: Thanks.
    Jessica: Can I get you anything? Would you like a drink?
  Nongluck: I'd love a glass of water.
    Jessica: And for you, Jolanta?
    Jolanta: (1) .... a cup of tea?
    Jessica: Yes, of course. How do you like it?
    Jolanta: White with two sugars, please.
    Jessica: (2) .... something to eat? Can I get you a biscuit?
    Jolanta: No, thanks.
    Jessica: How about you, Nongluck? (3) ....
  Nongluck: I'd like a biscuit, please. I love sweet things.

can I get   for you   can I get you

2   Assistant: Good morning.
      Anita: Hi, (4) .... a black coffee, please?
    Assistant: Sure, just one minute. And (5) .... anything else? A cake?
      Anita: No, thanks. I don't really like cakes.
    Assistant: And (6) .... ?
  Muhammad: Well, I like cakes a lot, but just a coffee for me too. Thanks, anyway.

5 Listen again and check.

6 Listen and practise.

Can I get you anything?   *Could I have a cup of tea?*   *Would you like something to eat?*
What can I get you?   *Can I get you anything else?*

7 Work in pairs. Choose a conversation from exercise 4 and practise.

12b A menu

Type of activity
Learners learn to read a menu and understand some labelling on food products. Individual and group work.

AECC reference
Rs/E1.1a, Rt/E1.1b, Rt/E1.2

Aims
Learners will learn to obtain information from texts and recognise that how a text looks can predict its purpose.

Language
understanding menus

Vocabulary
dessert, main course, starter; delicious, tasty, lovely

Preparation
Photocopy the worksheet. Take in menus from various places.

Differentiation
Weaker learners: dictate some food and drinks and ask them to write them under two groups: food or drink. Stronger learners: ask them to think of more foods to put into the starter, main course and dessert sections.

Warmer

Ask learners what kinds of British food they know, brainstorm these and write them on the board. Leave these on the board for exercise 2 then ask learners to read the menu and see if any of the items are on it.

1 Ask learners to look at the labels and match them with the sentences.

> **Answers**
> 1 b   2 a   3 c

2 Go over the words and ask them to complete the menu.

> **Answers**
> 1 starters   2 main courses   3 desserts

3 Ask learners to read the menu again and choose the answers.

> **Answers**
> 1 b   2 b   3 a   4 b   5 b

4 Ask learners to complete the sentences.

> **Answers**
> 1 lovely   2 healthy/low fat   3 delicious/lovely
> 4 tasty

5 Put learners into pairs and ask them to talk about the questions together.

Extension

Ask learners to write a conversation between the waiter / food server and customer(s).
Ask learners to work together and write their own menu.

Answers: Self-study exercises

A menu

Your own notes

1 2 lovely   3 delicious

2 2 a meal or a hot drink   3 8.15–10.30
4 4.45–7.15

A menu (12b)

1 Match the words with the sentences.

1 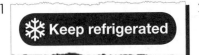 2 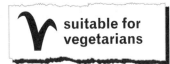 3 suitable for vegetarians

a Be careful – this food can make some people ill.
b Keep this food cold.
c There's no meat in this food.

2 Read and complete.

desserts   main courses   starters

Dearheart restaurant – *fixed three-course menu (£6.50)*

1 ....
Delicious vegetable or chicken soup

2 ....
Tasty beef and mushroom pie
Roast chicken* – healthy option (LF)
Omelette (v) – with: mushroom, cheese or peppers

Note: all meals are served with side dishes. Choose from:
• New potatoes or chips
• Vegetables or salad

3 ....
Delicious strawberry ice cream
Lovely apple pie with cream

Children's menu
Sausage, beans and chips
Fish fingers, peas and mashed potatoes

Extra portions
Chips (75p)
Rice (70p)
Onion rings (90p)

*halal/kosher options
(v) = vegetarian
(LF) = low fat

3 Read and answer.

1 You can have (a) two (b) three (c) four different kinds of omelette.
2 The low fat food is (a) beef pie (b) roast chicken (c) ice cream.
3 There (a) is (b) isn't a menu for children.
4 You (a) pay extra (b) don't pay for extra portions with the main meal.
5 You can buy extra (a) salad (b) rice (c) soup for your meal.

4 Find words in the menu to complete the sentences.

1 That ice cream is ......*lovely*...... .
2 Salad is .... food.
3 Thank you for the meal, it was ....
4 Chinese food is very .... I really like it.

5 Work together. Ask each other the questions.

1 What is the food like in your college restaurant?
2 What is your favourite British food?

12c A recipe

Type of activity
Learners read a short text then work together to write a recipe. Individual and pair work.

AECC reference
Ws/E1.1, Ww/E1.2

Aims
Learners will practise writing sentences using basic word order, imperative verb forms and basic punctuation.

Language
giving instructions; imperatives; countable and uncountable nouns; linking with *when*

Vocabulary
break, mix, add, pour, heat, fold, melt

Preparation
Photocopy the worksheet. Take in a bowl, whisk or fork and frying pan for exercise 2.

Differentiation
Weaker learners: teach more things we use for cooking or eating like *fork, spoon, knife*.
Stronger learners: ask them to write about their favourite food or their country's national dish and what ingredients we need to make it.

Warmer

Ask learners what their favourite food is. Then tell learners to ask each other and make a note of the answers. You could do this as a quick walk-round activity and collect the results of the survey on the board.

1 Go over the pictures and see if learners can describe what is happening in them. Tell them to use the pictures to complete the recipe.

> **Answers**
> 1 Break the eggs   2 mix the eggs   3 pour in
> 4 add   5 fold the omelette   6 Have a good meal

2 (▶37) Play the recording as learners read the text and check their answers. If you have brought in some of the kitchen implements, you could ask one or two learners to act out the actions on the recording.

3 Ask learners to decide which nouns are countable and which are uncountable.

> **Answers**
> countable: eggs, mushrooms
> uncountable: salt, pepper, butter, oil, milk, cheese

4 Put learners in pairs and ask them to complete the recipe for a pancake using words from the unit.

> **Answers**
> 1 Put   2 Add   3 add   4 heat   5 pour

Extension

Ask learners to cook a simple dish from their country to share with other learners and bring in the recipe for other learners.

Answers: Self-study exercises   **A recipe**   **Your own notes**

1 2 add   3 mix   4 heat   5 break   6 melt
2 2 C   3 U   4 C   5 U   6 C
3 2 heat   3 cook   4 Add   5 mix

A recipe (12c)

1 Look at the pictures and complete the recipe.

Making an omlette: steps 1–5

1   2   3   4   5

| add   fold the omelette   have a good meal   mix the eggs   pour in   break the eggs |

French omelette

Ingredients

2–3 fresh eggs per person   cheese, mushrooms or other fillings
milk   butter and oil
salt and pepper

Method: (1) .... into a bowl and add <u>salt</u> and <u>pepper</u>. Add a little <u>milk</u> and then
(2) .... with a fork. In a frying pan, add half a teaspoon of <u>butter</u> and oil.
Put it on the cooker and heat the butter and <u>oil</u>. When the butter melts and the oil is hot,
(3) .... the <u>eggs</u>. When the eggs are cooking, (4) .... the <u>cheese</u> or
<u>mushrooms</u> or another filling, and then (5) .... in half and serve. (6) .... !

2 Listen and do the actions.

3 Put the <u>underlined</u> words from the recipe into groups.

countable: ....
uncountable: ....

4 Work together. Complete the recipe.

| add   put   mix   pour   have   heat |

Pancakes

Ingredients

110g flour   milk and water
salt   oil
2 eggs

Serve with: lemon or orange juice and sugar

Method: (1) .... the flour into a bowl. (2) .... the eggs and the salt.
Slowly (3) .... the milk and water and mix them all together. In a frying pan,
(4) .... the oil and when it is hot (5) .... in some of the pancake mixture from
the bowl. Fry the pancake for two minutes on each side and serve with lemon juice and sugar.
(6) .... a nice meal!

13a The weather

Type of activity
Learners listen to sounds and then practise a conversation. Individual and pair work.

AECC reference
Sc/E1.4a, Sc/E1.4d, Lr/E1.2e

Aims
Learners will practise making simple statements of fact and giving a description.

Language
talking about the weather; present continuous affirmative

Vocabulary
winter, spring, autumn, summer; rain/rainy, wind/windy, sun/sunny, stormy, fog, snow, ice

Preparation
Photocopy the worksheet. Take in flashcards or photos of different kinds of weather.

Differentiation
Weaker learners: ask them to make adjectives from *sun, ice, fog*.
Stronger learners: ask them to add more actions to exercise 6 so that they can tell their partner to perform them.

Warmer

Ask learners what the weather is like today, and if they like the weather in the UK – why or why not?

1 Tell learners to label the pictures then practise the pronunciation of the words with them.

> **Answers**
> 1 winter   2 spring   3 autumn   4 summer

2 Go over the words and practise the pronunciation. Ask learners to match the words with the pictures.

> **Answers**
> wind picture 3   sun picture 4   fog picture 3
> snow/ice picture 1

3 (▶38) Tell learners to listen to the sounds and write the kind of weather they hear. Point out the difference between nouns and adjectives for weather: e.g. *rain – rainy*.

> **Answers**
> 1 rainy   2 stormy   3 windy   4 snowy

4 (▶39) Play the recording as learners listen and order the sentences.

> **Answers**
> 1 It's raining.   2 He's driving.   3 He's walking.
> 4 He's getting his keys.   5 He's opening the door.
> 6 He's taking his raincoat off.   7 He's sitting down.

5 (▶39) Play the recording as learners listen and do the actions.

6 Put learners in pairs and ask them to say the sentences for their partner to perform.

7 (▶40) Tell learners to cover up exercise 8. Ask learners to listen to the conversation and tick a, b or c.

> **Answers**
> 1 a   2 c   3 b

8 (▶40) Tell learners to listen again and complete the sentences as they listen.

> **Answers**
> 1 look   2 like   3 Don't worry   4 kind

9 (▶41) Play the recording as learners practise the phrases.

10 Put learners in pairs and ask them to change the conversation using the weather in their own country or the town where they live now. Ask them to perform their new conversation for the class.

Extension

Ask learners to look at a newspaper weather forecast and write two or three sentences about it, e.g. *It's raining in Scotland.*

Answers: Self-study exercises ⟩ **The weather** ⟨ **Your own notes**

1 2 sunny   3 windy   4 icy   5 stormy
2 2 cold   3 dear   4 raincoat   5 Don't worry

The weather (13a)

1 Label the pictures.

| autumn spring summer winter |

1 .... 2 .... 3 .... 4 ....

2 Match the words with the pictures.

rain ....*picture 2*....   fog ....   sun ....

wind ....   snow/ice ....

3 Listen and write.

| rainy snowy stormy windy |

1 It's .... today.   3 It's .... today.
2 It's .... today.   4 It's .... today.

4 Listen and order the sentences.

A He's sitting down. ....   E He's opening the door. ....
B He's driving. ....   F He's taking his raincoat off. ....
C It's raining. ....*1*..........   G He's getting his keys. ....
D He's walking. ....

5 Listen again and do the actions.

6 Work together. Say sentences from exercise 4 for your partner to do.

You're driving.

7 Listen to a conversation and tick (✓) the correct answer.

1 What's the weather like? (a) Rainy. ☐ (b) Sunny. ☐ (c) Windy. ☐

2 Natasha doesn't have (a) a coat. ☐ (b) an umbrella ☐ (c) a hat. ☐

3 Khaled gives Natasha his (a) raincoat ☐ (b) umbrella ☐ (c) raincoat and umbrella. ☐

8 Listen again and complete.

| don't worry kind look like |

Natasha: Oh, (1) .... outside.
  Khaled: Why? What's the weather (2) .... ?
Natasha: It's raining and I don't have an umbrella.
  Khaled: (3) .... – you can have my umbrella. I'm wearing my raincoat today.
Natasha: Oh, thank you – that's very (4) ....

9 Listen and practise.

Look outside.   What's the weather like?   Don't worry.   That's very kind.

10 Work together. Change the conversation in exercise 8 and practise.

From *ESOL Activities Entry 1* © Cambridge University Press 2008 **PHOTOCOPIABLE**

13b Great British weather

Type of activity
Learners read about weather conditions in the UK and listen to a weather forecast. Individual and pair work.

AECC reference
Rs/E1.1a, Rt/E1.1a

Aims
Learners will practise reading a short narrative on a familiar topic and practise reading for detail.

Language
talking about the weather; *generally, around, about*

Vocabulary
points of the compass; *warm, cool, wet, mild, cold*

Preparation
Photocopy the worksheet. Take in a map of the UK, and weather forecasting symbols.

Differentiation
Weaker learners: play *Odd One Out* with words from the worksheet, e.g.
cold   warm   rain   hot
Stronger learners: ask them to look at another weather forecast in that day's newspaper and write a few sentences about it.

Warmer

Put learners into groups and ask them to think of as many types of weather as they can in three minutes. At the end of three minutes, get feedback from the groups and write their answers on the board.

1 Tell learners to look at the picture and complete the points of the compass.

> **Answers**
> 1 west   2 east   3 south

2 Tell learners to label the pictures. Practise the pronunciation of the words.

> **Answers**
> 1 stormy   2 showery   3 cloudy   4 foggy

3 Ask learners to read the text and complete the table.

> **Answers**
>
> | | months | temperature | weather |
> |---|---|---|---|
> | spring | March–May | 6–11 °C | sunny, cool, showery |
> | summer | June–August | 14–30 °C | warm, hot days, cool evenings |
> | autumn | September–November | 7–18 °C | warm or cool, foggy |
> | winter | December–February | 1–5 °C | cold, icy |

4 Tell learners to read the text again and answer the questions.

> **Answers**
> 1 One day in three.
> 2 Because Britain is in the north.
> 3 Seven or eight hours.

5 Ask learners to draw a map of their country and write a few sentences about the weather, seasons and geography in their country.

Extension

Put learners' maps and descriptions from exercise 5 on the wall and let the other learners walk round and read about other learners' countries.

Answers: Self-study exercises   **Great British weather**   **Your own notes**

1 1 North   2 East   3 South   4 West

2 1 warm   2 mild   3 cool

3 1 dry with sunshine
　　2 cloudy
　　3 wind from the south-west

Great British weather (13b)

1 Complete.

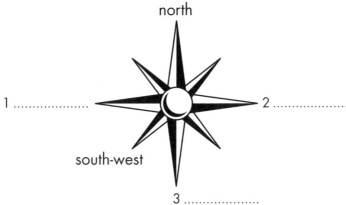

north

1 ....   2 ....

south-west

3 ....

2 Label the pictures.

| cloudy   foggy   showery   stormy |

1 ....   2 ....   3 ....   4 ....

3 Read and complete the table.

	months	temperature	weather
spring			sunny, cool, wet
summer	June–August		
autumn			
winter		1–5 °C	

The weather in Britain

Many people think Britain is wet and cold. It rains about one day in three in England and the wind generally comes from the south-west. Generally, Britain has mild weather – we have long evenings in summer because Britain is in the north and we can have good weather in all seasons.

In spring (March–May), we have sunny weather, but it can also be cool or showery. Temperatures are around 6–11 °C. Generally, days in summer are warm, but evenings can be cool. Temperatures are about 14–30 °C, but it can be up to 35 °C. In autumn (September–November), there can be very warm days, but there can be cool days – it can be foggy with temperatures at around 7–18 °C. In December, January and February days are short and cold and it can be icy, with about seven or eight hours of daylight.

4 Read again and answer.

1 On how many days does it rain in England? ....
2 Why are summer evenings long and warm? ....
3 How many hours of daylight do we have in winter? ....

5 Draw a map of your country. Write about the seasons and the weather.

In the winter it can be very cold in the north of my country.

13c Clothes

Type of activity
Learners read a magazine article, complete a table and write a short text about themselves. Individual and pair work.

AECC reference
Wt/E1.1, Ws/E1.1

Aims
Learners will practise writing a short description about themselves with correct order of adjectives.

Language
describing clothes; basic order of adjectives (age, colour and material)

Vocabulary
jacket, coat, hoodie, trousers, sandals, jumper, boots, hat, shorts, scarf

Preparation
Photocopy the worksheet. Take in different kinds of clothes.

Differentiation
Weaker learners: say some items of clothing and tell learners to point to them, if anyone is wearing them. Stronger learners: ask them to look for other adjectives in the text about clothes: *light, comfortable*, and try to think of the opposites for these.

Warmer

On the board write: *1 head/neck, 2 body, 3 feet*. Put learners into groups and give them five minutes to write down as many clothes as they can for each part of the body. If you brought in more clothes, you could pre-teach these now.

1 Tell learners to write the words under the pictures.

> **Answers**
> 1 T-shirt   2 coat   3 hoodie   4 socks   5 sandals
> 6 jumper   7 boots   8 hat   9 shorts   10 scarf
> 11 slippers   12 trousers

2 Tell learners to read the text and answer the questions. You may want to revise colours: *blue, red, black;* and materials: *cotton, wool, leather*.

> **Answers**
> 1 light, comfortable clothes – shorts, T-shirt and sandals
> 2 a red cotton hoodie, a T-shirt and slippers
> 3 Because she can wear her coat and scarves.

3 Ask learners to read the text again and complete the table.

> **Answers**
> summer: 1 T-shirt   2 hoodie   3 slippers   4 cotton
>   5 blue
> winter: 1 scarves   2 boots   3 wool   4 red
>   5 black

4 Put learners in pairs. Ask them to sit back-to-back and try to remember what their partner is wearing. Prompt them if necessary with questions about the colour and material of their partner's clothing and make sure they are using the present continuous third person correctly.

5 Ask learners to write about what they are wearing or what their partner is wearing, paying attention to the order of adjectives.

Extension

Ask learners to write about the clothes they like wearing in summer and winter, or at home and at work, college or outside.

Answers: Self-study exercises   **Clothes**   **Your own notes**

1 2 Comfortable leather shoes
   3 Old red slippers
   4 A fashionable blue hoodie

2 2 hats   3 a pair of shorts   4 a pair of trousers
   5 jumpers   6 scarves

Clothes 13c

1 Label the pictures.

| boots | coat | hat | hoodie | trousers | jumper | sandals | scarf | shorts | slippers | socks | T-shirt |

1 .... 2 .... 3 .... 4 .... 5 .... 6 ....

7 .... 8 .... 9 .... 10 .... 11 .... 12 ....

2 Read and answer the questions.

We ask TV star Zenia Griffin what she's wearing now and what she likes to wear.

Summer

Today I'm wearing my light, comfortable clothes. I'm wearing a pair of black cotton shorts and a blue T-shirt. I'm also wearing a pair of leather sandals. In the evening, I wear my red cotton hoodie, my T-shirt and my old slippers.

Winter

I love winter because I can wear my coat and winter scarves. When it's really cold I wear my wool jumper and thick wool socks. And when it snows – that's great – I put on my red boots and my black hat!

1 What clothes is she wearing? ....
2 What does she wear in the evening in summer? ....
3 Why does she like winter weather? ....

3 Read again and complete.

summer				
clothes / shoes	shorts	(1) ...T-shirt...	sandals	(2) ....
material	(3)		leather	cotton
colour	black	(4)		red

winter					
clothes / shoes	coat	(1)	jumper	socks	(2)	hat
material			(3)	wool		
colour					(4)	(5) ....

4 Work together. Turn round and say what your partner is wearing.

5 Write about what you are wearing today or what your partner is wearing.

Today I'm wearing my …

14a At the doctor's

Type of activity
Learners complete a crossword then practise a conversation. Individual and pair work.

AECC reference
Sd/E1.1b, Lr/E1.2c, Lr/E1.3a

Aims
Learners will practise making an appointment and describing symptoms.

Language
making an appointment; describing symptoms; *have got*

Vocabulary
back, foot, shoulder, mouth, throat, arm, head; feel sick, cold, cough, stomach ache, back ache, sore throat; appointments, prescription

Preparation
Photocopy the worksheet. Take in a picture of a person.

Differentiation
Weaker learners: dictate some of the words from exercise 1 like *stomach*, *shoulder*, *mouth* and *throat*.
Stronger learners: ask them to make another crossword using words for parts of the body.

Warmer

Play 'Simon Says' with words for parts of the body. If you have brought in a picture, you could use this to teach more words.

1 Tell learners to complete the crossword and find the missing word. Practise the pronunciation of the words.

Answers

		¹s	h	o	u	l	d	e	r
²f	o	o	t						
³t	h	r	o	a	t				
			⁴m	o	u	t	h		
			⁵a	r	m				
	⁶b	a	c	k					
		⁷h	e	a	d				

2 Ask learners to look at the pictures and match the sentences. Practise the sentences.

Answers
1 I've got a cold.
2 I've got a stomach ache.
3 I've got backache.
4 I've got a cough.
5 I feel sick.
6 My throat is sore.

3 (▶42) Play the recording and ask learners to practise the sentences.

4 (▶43) Tell learners to cover up exercise 5. Then ask them to listen to the conversations and tick the sentences they hear.

Answers
I've got a stomach ache. ✓   My throat is sore. ✓

5 (▶43) Play the conversations one by one again and tell learners to complete them using the words in the boxes.

Answers
1 appointments   2 doctor   3 stomach ache
4 matter   5 anything   6 prescription

6 Put learners in pairs and ask them to choose and practise one of the conversations.

Extension

Ask learners to write another short conversation, changing the illnesses, names and so on.

Answers: Self-study exercises   **At the doctor's**   **Your own notes**

1 2 shoulder   3 mouth   4 throat

2 2 stomach ache   3 headache   4 sore throat

3 2 sore   3 Let   4 anything   5 prescription

At the doctor's 14a

1 Complete the crossword and find the word.

| arm | back | foot | head | mouth | shoulder | throat |

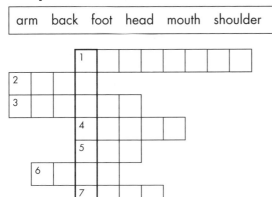

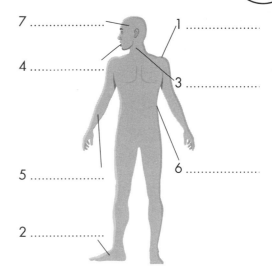

2 Match the sentences with the pictures.

I feel sick.   I've got a cold.   I've got a cough.   I've got a stomach ache.
I've got backache.   My throat is sore.

1 .... 2 .... 3 .... 4 .... 5 .... 6 ....

3 Listen and practise.

4 Listen to two conversations and tick (✓) the sentences in exercise 2 that you hear.

5 Listen again and complete.

1 Receptionist: Good morning. How can I help you?
     Sharif: Have you got any free (1) .... today?
  Receptionist: Who is your (2) .... ?
     Sharif: My doctor's name is Hu. Dr Hu.
  Receptionist: OK. There's an appointment for three o'clock. Is that OK?
     Sharif: Do you have any for this morning? I've got a really bad (3) ....
  Receptionist: There's an appointment with Dr Livingstone at 11.30.
     Sharif: OK, 11.30 with Dr Livingstone.

> doctor
> appointments
> stomach ache

2 Dr Livingstone: Hello. Come in and sit down. I'm Dr Livingstone.
       Sharif: Hello.
  Dr Livingstone: How can I help you? What's the (4) .... ?
       Sharif: I've got a stomach ache and my throat is sore.
  Dr Livingstone: I see. Are you taking (5) .... for this?
       Sharif: No, doctor.
  Dr Livingstone: OK, let me have a look at your throat. Uh-huh.
       Sharif: Is it bad?
  Dr Livingstone: No, not really. Take this (6) .... to the chemist. Come back to see me
            next week.
       Sharif: Thank you very much.

> anything
> matter
> prescription

6 Work together. Practise one of the conversations.

14b Medicine labels

Type of activity
Learners practise reading instructions and information on a medicine packet.

AECC reference
Rs/E1.1a, Rt/E1.1b

Aims
Learners will practise obtaining information for texts.

Language
How much … ? / How many … ?

Vocabulary
tablet, capsule, cream, powder, medicine; recommended, dosage, external, directions, warning

Preparation
Photocopy the worksheet. Take in different medicines from the chemist's.

Differentiation
Weaker learners: tell them to cover the words in exercise 1 and write them again with correct spelling.
Stronger learners: ask them to read the text again and say what information is on the front of a medicine packet.

Warmer

Give learners some cards with the illnesses on them: *stomach ache, cough, headache, backache,* and so on. Put them into groups and ask them to mime the illness to the group. The learner who gets the answer first gets a point.

1 Ask learners to match the words with the pictures. Practise the pronunciation of the words.

> **Answers**
> 1 tablets   2 capsules   3 medicine   4 powder
> 5 cream

2 Ask learners to read the text and match the questions with the information.

> **Answers**
> 1 a   2 d   3 b   4 c

3 Tell learners to read the packet and answer the questions.

> **Answers**
> 1 16 capsules
> 2 headache, toothache, sore throat
> 3 with a glass of water
> 4 No
> 5 eight

4 Put learners in pairs and tell them to ask each other the questions.

Extension

Ask learners to bring in an empty medicine packet from a chemist's and explain what it is used for, who it is recommended for, the dosage and the directions for use.

Answers: Self-study exercises   **Medicine labels**   **Your own notes**

1 2 capsule   3 cream   4 powder   5 medicine
2 1 coughs, colds and sore throat   2 yes   3 six

Medicine labels 14b

1 Label the pictures.

capsules	cream	medicine	powder	tablets

 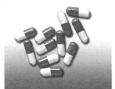   

1 .... 2 .... 3 .... 4 .... 5 ....

2 Read the text and match 1–4 with a–d.

1 How many can you have?
2 Who cannot take it?
3 What is it for?
4 In your mouth or on your skin?

a dosage
b recommended for
c external use only
d warning

Medicine labels

In the UK all medicines have clear labels. On the front of the packet is the name of the medicine and why we use it. We can also see if the medicine is in tablets, capsules or a cream.

Important information is on the back of the packet:

recommended for – why we use it – for example, headache, sore throat.

dosage – how many tablets you can take in one day and who can take this – children, adults or old people.

for external use only means you cannot eat or drink the medicine – you can only use it on your body.

warning – who cannot use the medicine.

---

3 Read and answer.

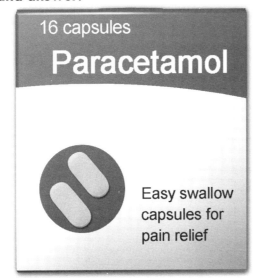

16 capsules
Paracetamol

Easy swallow
capsules for
pain relief

Recommended for		
Headache	Toothache	Sore throat
Directions Swallow the capsule with a glass of water		

Age	Dosage
Adults, Children over 12	2 capsules, 4 times a day
Children under 12	Not recommended

⚠ WARNING.
No more than 8 capsules
in 24 hours

Not for children under 12.

1 How much of the medicine is there?
2 What can you use the medicine for?
3 How do you take the medicine?

4 Can a ten-year-old child take this?
5 How many capsules can you take in 24 hours?

4 Work together. Answer the questions.

1 Do you take medicines?
2 What do you do when you have a headache?
3 What do you do when you have a cold?

14c An absence note

Type of activity
Learners practise writing a note of absence, apologising and excusing.

AECC reference
Ws/E1.1, Ws/E1.3

Aims
Learners will practise writing a simple text to communicate basic information.

Language
saying sorry, wishing someone well; present continuous affirmative and negative

Vocabulary
a temperature, get well soon, get better soon

Preparation
Photocopy the worksheet.

Differentiation
Weaker learners: mime some illnesses like *cold, cough, headache* and ask them to guess the illness.
Stronger learners: ask them to underline all the instances of the present continuous in the texts.

---

1 Ask learners to look at the pictures and say what they can see. Then ask them to read notes A and B and match them with the pictures.

> **Answers**
> 1 A   2 B

2 Tell learners to read the notes again and match them with the replies.

> **Answers**
> A + D; B + C

3 Ask learners to answer the questions.

> **Answers**
> 1 He has a headache and a temperature.
> 2 He has a bad cough.
> 3 Pinar
> 4 a doctor's note

4 Tell learners to put the phrases into groups. Then practise the pronunciation of the phrases.

> **Answers**
> 1 Please excuse me, I'm sorry but I can't come to class today
> 2 get better soon, get well soon

5 Go over the writing frame and ask them to use it to write a note.

Extension

Ask learners to write an absence note for themselves.

Answers: Self-study exercises   **An absence note**   **Your own notes**

1 2 I'm sorry but I can't come   3 Get well soon
2 2 is taking care   3 am lying   4 am reading
   5 am not enjoying

An absence note (14c)

1 Read and match the notes with the pictures.

A

Dear Teacher,

I'm sorry but I can't come to class today. I am not feeling very well at the moment. I have a headache and a temperature and I am waiting for an appointment with the doctor.

Saqib

B

Dear Mr Noble,

Please excuse me today. My son has a bad cough and I am taking care of him today. Please send me the homework.

Many thanks,

Irshad

1

2

2 Read the notes again and match them with the replies.

C

Dear Irshad,

I'm sorry that your son is not well. Pinar is bringing your homework to you later today. I hope your son gets better soon.

Best wishes,

Tom Noble

D

Dear Saqib,

Don't worry about it. Could you get a note from the doctor for the college office?

Get well soon,

Tom Noble

3 Read again and answer the questions.

1 What is wrong with Saqib? ....
2 What is wrong with Irshad's son? ....
3 Who is bringing Irshad's homework? ....
4 What does Tom want from Saqib? ....

4 Put the phrases into groups.

| get better soon   get well soon   I'm sorry but I can't come to class today   Please excuse me |

1 saying sorry: ....
2 hoping someone gets well: ....

5 Write a note.

Dear .... ,

Please excuse me I'm sorry	but I can't	meet you see you come	today this afternoon this morning	because
I have (got) a	bad terrible	cough. cold. headache.	Can you please	
send email	me	the homework?		

15a Sending a parcel

Type of activity
Learners listen to conversations in a Post Office then practise a conversation. Individual and pair work.

AECC reference
Sc/E1.2a, Sd/E1.1b, Lr/E1.5c

Aims
Learners will practise speaking and listening in simple exchanges in everyday contexts.

Language
making requests; *Can I / can you … ?*, *Could you … ?*, *Have you got … ?*

Vocabulary
stamp, scales, gas card, envelope, parcel

Preparation
Photocopy the worksheet. Take in stamps, letters and parcels.

Differentiation
Weaker learners: after they have completed exercise 3, choose a conversation again and play it again line by line, stopping after each line for learners to write it down until they have the complete conversation.
Stronger learners: ask them what they can buy or do in a Post Office.

Warmer
Play 'Hangman' with some of the words presented in the worksheet such as *envelope, stamp, scales, parcel*. If you have brought in items from the post office, use these to pre-teach the vocabulary.

1 Ask learners to label the pictures. Practise the pronunciation.

> **Answers**
> 1 stamp   2 scales   3 envelope   4 parcel

2 (▶44) Tell learners to cover up exercise 3. Ask them to listen and write Yes or No.

> **Answers**
> 1 No (a first-class stamp)
> 2 Yes
> 3 No (to London)

3 (▶44) Ask learners to listen to the recording again and complete the questions.

> **Answers**
> 1 everything   2 got   3 put   4 Could you
> 5 Could you   6 is that

4 (▶45) Play the recording and practise the pronunciation.

5 Put learners in pairs and ask them to practise one of the conversations with their partner.

Extension
Ask learners to write another short conversation about topping up a mobile phone or putting money on an electricity card.

Answers: Self-study exercises   **Sending a parcel**   **Your own notes**

1 2 What can I do for you?
  3 Could you put it on the scales?
  4 Have you got a second-class stamp?

2 1 second-class stamp   2 all   3 envelope

Sending a parcel 15a

1 Label the pictures.

| envelope   parcel   scales   stamp |

1 .... 2 .... 3 .... 4 ....

2 Listen to three conversations. Write Yes or No.

conversation 1   The person is buying a second-class stamp. ....

conversation 2   The person is paying for gas. ....

conversation 3   The person wants to send the parcel out of the country. ....

3 Listen again. Complete the questions.

| could you   everything   got   is that   put   could you |

1   Customer A: Can I have a first-class stamp, please?
    Assistant: Yes, here you are. Is that (1) .... ?
    Customer A: Have you (2) .... an envelope?
    Assistant: No, we don't sell envelopes.

2   Assistant: Hello. What can I do for you?
    Customer B: Can you (3) .... £5.00 on my gas card, please?
    Assistant: (4) .... put your card in the machine, please?
    Customer B: OK.
    Assistant: There you go, madam. £5.00 gas.

3   Assistant: (5) .... put the parcel on the scales, please?
    Customer C: OK.
    Assistant: And (6) .... international or national?
    Customer C: It's to London.
    Assistant: So that's £2.46 first class.

4 Listen and practise the questions.

Can I have a first-class stamp, please?
Have you got an envelope?
Can you put £5.00 on my gas card, please?

5 Work together. Choose a conversation from exercise 3 and practise.

15b Special Delivery

Type of activity
Learners read instructions. Individual and pair work.

AECC reference
Rw/E1.1, Rw/E1.3b, Rt/E1.1b

Aims
Learners will practise following a short narrative on a familiar topic.

Language
sequencing words: *then, next, first, now*

Vocabulary
receive, send, stick, weigh; first-/second-class, special delivery

Preparation
Photocopy the worksheet. Take in first- and second-class stamps and special delivery forms.

Differentiation
Weaker learners: go over the spelling rules in exercise 4, then dictate the words to them and ask them to write them with correct spelling.
Stronger learners: tell them to read the text again and underline the words like *first* and *next* for sequencing instructions.

Warmer

Put learners into groups and dictate some of the words from the worksheet to them: *letter, parcel, special, delivery, address.* They should write them down with correct spelling. The group with the most correctly spelled words is the winner.

1 Ask learners to match the words with the pictures. Practise the pronunciation of the words.

Answers
1 weigh   2 send   3 receive   4 stick

2 Ask learners to read the text and choose the correct option.

Answers
1 b   2 c   3 a

3 Ask learners to read the text again and order the pictures.

Answers
a 5   b 1   c 4   d 3   e 2

4 Tell learners that in many English words *i* comes before *e* when they are together, but for some words *e* comes before *i*. Tell learners to complete the words.

Answers
1 eight   2 weigh   3 neighbour   4 their   5 receive

5 Put learners in pairs and tell them to ask each other the questions. At the end of the exercise get the answers from one or two pairs.

Extension

Ask learners what other forms they can find in the post office.

Answers: Self-study exercises

Special Delivery

Your own notes

1 2 send   3 stick   4 weigh
2 1 C   2 B   3 D   4 A

Special Delivery (15b)

1 Match the words with the pictures.

receive   send   stick   weigh

  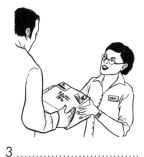 

1 ....   2 ....   3 ....   4 ....

2 Read and tick (✓).

1 A first-class letter arrives …

(a) before 1 pm the next day. ☐   (b) one to two days later. ☐   (c) two to three days later. ☐

2 A second-class letter arrives …

(a) before 1 pm the next day. ☐   (b) one to two days later. ☐   (c) two to three days later. ☐

3 A Special Delivery letter arrives …

(a) before 1 pm the next day. ☐   (b) one to two days later. ☐   (c) two to three days later. ☐

Royal Mail Special Delivery

At the Post Office you can send letters and parcels in different ways. First-class post takes one to two working days. Second-class post takes two to three working days. And Special Delivery is for important things.

When you send something by Special Delivery, first you write the person's address on the front of the parcel and your address on the back. Then you take it to the Post Office. Tell the assistant that you want to use Special Delivery. Next show them the address, and then put the parcel on the scales so they can weigh it. Then give the parcel to the assistant, and say how much it is worth. They will check you have put your address on the parcel. Then they will give you a receipt for your parcel. Special Delivery gets there before lunch the next working day.

3 Read again and order the pictures.

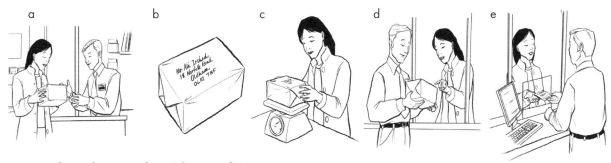

a   b   c   d   e

4 Complete the words with e and i.

1 …*ei*.ght   2 w……gh   3 n……ghbour   4 th……r   5 rec……ve

5 Ask each other the questions.

1 Do you send a lot of letters? Do you send a lot of parcels?
2 Do you send things abroad or in the UK?
3 Do you use Special Delivery? Why (not)?

15c Thank you

Type of activity
Learners read short letters and notes and write a thank you note. Individual work.

AECC reference
Ww/E1.1a, Ws/E1.1

Aims
Learners will practise constructing simple sentences.

Language
phrases for giving and receiving presents; *What a +
adjective ... !*

Vocabulary
adjectives to express pleasure or approval: *great, lovely,
nice; gift, present*

Preparation
Photocopy the worksheet.

Differentiation
Weaker learners: write up some of the phrases from
the unit with wrong word order on the board, e.g.
present you for thank the lovely, and ask them to write
them again in the correct order.
Stronger learners: ask them to underline the ways of
offering a gift: *When I saw this I thought of you. /
Here's a small gift for you.*

Warmer

Practise the phrase *What a lovely/great/nice* + object by
getting a learner to give you their pen/book/ruler. Then
put learners into pairs and ask them to exchange items
and say the phrase.

1 Ask learners to say when they write notes, e.g. to
thank someone, to say they will be absent from class.
Ask learners which notes are emails, texts or letters.

> **Answers**
> 1 A and D   2 C and B

2 Ask learners to read the notes and write the names of
the people.

> **Answers**
> A Maryam   B Ahmed   C Amina   D Satar

3 Ask learners to read the notes again and answer the
questions.

> **Answers**
> 1 Satar   2 Maryam   3 (My) Dear
> 4 Love, Yours, Best wishes

4 Ask learners to write the words in the correct column in
the table.

> **Answers**
> 1 nice   2 great   3 inviting / helping
> 4 helping / inviting   5 enjoy

5 Tell learners to write a note to Amina thanking her for
giving them a CD.

Answers: Self-study exercises   Thank you   Your own notes

1 2 lovely   3 great   4 nice

2 2 nice
   3 great
   4 lovely

3 Own answers

Thank you 15c

1 Look at the messages and say which are about (1) giving and which are about (2) receiving a present.

A

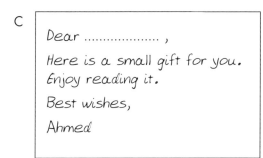

Dear .... ,

When I saw this, I thought of you. Hope you like the music!

Love,

Satar

B

My dear .... ,

Thank you for the lovely present!
I love books.

Yours,

Amina

C

Dear .... ,

Here is a small gift for you. Enjoy reading it.

Best wishes,

Ahmed

D

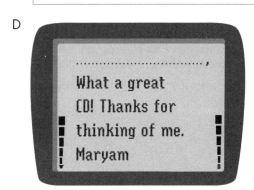

.... ,
What a great CD! Thanks for thinking of me. Maryam

2 Read and complete the notes with the names of the people.

3 Read again and answer the questions.

1 Who sent a CD? ....

2 ... and who received it? ....

3 How can you start a letter? ....

4 ... and how can you finish it? ....

4 Complete the table.

enjoy	great	helping	inviting	~~nice~~

What a	lovely	CD!
	(1) *nice*.........	gift!
	(2)	present!

Thanks for	thinking of	me!
	(3)	
	(4)	

Hope you	like	it.
	(5)	

5 Amina gave you a CD. Write a short note to thank her.

Dear ...

16a After you

Type of activity
Learners listen to conversations in various situations then practise them. Individual and pair work.

AECC reference
Sd/E1.1a, Lr/E1.4a, Lr/E1.5a

Aims
Learners will practise speaking and listening in simple exchanges in everyday contexts.

Language
polite social expressions

Vocabulary
excuse me, sorry, pardon me, queue, not at all, is this seat free, thanks anyway, you're welcome, after you

Preparation
Photocopy the worksheet.

Differentiation
Weaker learners: write queue, excuse, seat and anyway on the board, taking out the vowels, and ask learners to write in the missing letters.
Stronger learners: ask where they might see the signs in exercise 1 and why they are there, e.g. sign 4 is to let people who are in a hurry go past you on escalators.

Warmer
Play 'Hangman' with some of the phrases from the unit like Excuse me, Pardon me, You're welcome.

1 Tell learners to match the signs with the sentences.

> **Answers**
> 1 stand up for old people
> 2 wait in a line here
> 3 wait here
> 4 stand on the right

2 (▶46) Tell learners to cover up exercises 3 and 4. Then ask them to listen and match the conversations with the pictures.

> **Answers**
> A 3　B 1　C 2　D 4

3 (▶46) Play the recording again and ask learners to complete the conversations.

> **Answers**
> 1 the end　2 Excuse me　3 Not at all
> 4 thanks anyway　5 free　6 welcome　7 after you

4 (▶47) Play the recording and ask learners to practise the phrases.

5 Put learners in pairs. Ask learners to choose one or two of the conversations and practise them.

Extension
Ask learners to write a short conversation using some of the phrases.

Answers: Self-study exercises　　After you　　Your own notes

1 2 you　3 me　4 you

2 2 Is this seat free?
3 Would you like to sit here?
4 Is this seat free?

3 2 free　3 sorry　4 anyway　5 me　6 free　7 thanks

1 Match the words with the signs.

| stand on the right   stand up for old people   wait here   wait in a line here |

1 ....   2 ....   3 ....   4 ....

2 Listen and match the conversations with the pictures.

A   B   C   D

1 ....   2 ....   3 ....   4 ....

3 Listen again and complete the conversations.

| the end   free   after you   thanks anyway   not at all   excuse me   welcome |

1   Monika: Pardon me, is this (1) .... of the queue?
     Man 1: Yes, it is.

2   Khaled: (2) .... , would you like to sit here?
     Man 2: Oh, thank you very much.
     Khaled: (3) .... I'm getting off soon.

3   Isra: Excuse me, is this seat free?
     Man 3: I'm sorry, someone's sitting there.
        Isra: OK – (4) .... Excuse me, is this seat (5) .... ?
   Woman: Yes, it is. Please take it.
        Isra: Oh, thanks very much.
   Woman: You're (6) ....

4   Ahmed: After you.
     Man 4: No, no – (7) ....
     Ahmed: No, no – you first.
     Man 4: No, please, you first ...

4 Listen and practise.

| Pardon me. | After you. | | Is this seat free? | You're welcome. |
| Excuse me. | Is this the end of the queue? | | Thanks anyway. | Not at all. |

5 Work together. Choose a conversation in exercise 3 and practise it.

16b Good manners

Type of activity
Learners complete a quiz then read and check their answers. Individual and pair work.

AECC reference
Rs/E1.1a, Rt/E1.1b

Aims
Learners will practise reading a short text on a familiar topic.

Language
talking about customs and manners; *when* + subject + verb

Vocabulary
sneeze, kiss, shake hands, knock

Preparation
Photocopy the worksheet.

Differentiation
Weaker learners: ask them what they do when they meet someone they don't know, what they do when they see a queue or what they do when an old(er) person gets onto a crowded bus.
Stronger learners: ask them to make all the sentences in exercise 2 true, e.g. *When you meet someone, kiss them.* ➜ *When you meet someone, don't kiss them – shake their hand.*

Warmer

Mime some actions like *sneeze, shake hands, knock on a door* for learners and have them try to guess the words. You could turn it into a game by giving points for correct answers.

1 Ask learners for some examples of good manners and bad manners. Tell them to describe the pictures using the verbs.

> **Answers**
> 1 knock   2 shake hands   3 kiss   4 sneeze

2 Tell learners to read the quiz and decide if the sentences are true, sometimes true or not true in the UK. Tell them to cover the key with a piece of paper as they read.

3 Put learners in pairs and ask them to compare their answers.

4 Tell learners to read the key and check their answers.

5 Ask learners to work in groups and discuss which things in the quiz are good or bad manners or what other things are considered good or bad.

Extension

Ask learners to tell you or write a few sentences about other customs or habits they have noticed in the UK.

Answers: Self-study exercises   **Good manners**   **Your own note**

1   2 They're shaking hands.
    3 They're kissing.
    4 He's sneezing.

2   2 when someone does something bad
    3 when we don't hear something
    4 when we want someone to say something again
    5 when we feel sorry

Good manners 16b

1 Match the words with the pictures.

kiss knock shake hands sneeze

1 ....

2 ....

3 ....

4 ....

2 Read the quiz and tick (✓).

In the UK, people …	true	sometimes true	not true
1 kiss when they meet.			
2 stand up for old people on buses.			
3 call people by Mr(s) + first name (e.g. Mr Mike).			
4 don't say anything when they are late.			
5 knock on the door before they go into someone's room.			
6 ask how much other people earn.			
7 ask someone how old they are.			
8 shake everyone's hand when they go into a room.			
9 open doors for other people and let them go in first.			
10 sneeze without a handkerchief.			

3 Work together. Talk about your answers.

I think number 1 is sometimes true.

4 Read and check your answers.

1 Sometimes true – men and women kiss, but men don't kiss men.
2 Sometimes true – it's polite to stand up for old people on busy buses or trains.
3 Not true – we use *Mr(s)* + last name.
4 Not true – it's polite to say *Sorry I'm late.*
5 True – it's polite to knock on the door and wait for the person to say *Come in.*
6 Not true – don't ask someone how much they earn – it's not polite.
7 Not true – don't ask a person their age – it's not good manners.
8 Not true – just say *Hello.*
9 Sometimes true.
10 Not true – try to use a handkerchief when you sneeze.

5 Work in groups. Say which things are true in your country too.

16c A card for you

Type of activity
Learners read different types of cards then write their own. Individual work.

AECC reference
Rw/E1.2, Wt/E1.1, Ww/E1.1a

Aims
Learners will practise using and spelling some personal key words and composing a simple text to communicate ideas.

Language
expressions for different social occasions

Vocabulary
Mother's Day, congratulations, special

Preparation
Photocopy the worksheet. Take in folded card for learners to make and write their own cards.

Differentiation
Weaker learners: write more rhyming words on the board and ask them to match them, e.g.
sky, see, I, tea, lie, the
Stronger learners: ask them to try to write the rhyme for a birthday card.

Warmer

Write some words that rhyme on the board and ask learners to find the rhyming words, e.g. *right, tell, sun, light, well, fun,* and so on.

1 Ask learners who sends cards and why they send them. Ask learners to write the greetings on the front of the cards.

> **Answers**
> 1 Congratulations on your new baby
> 2 For a special mum
> 3 Happy wedding day

2 Tell learners to match the rhyming words.

> **Answers**
> 1 b   2 a   3 d   4 c

3 Ask learners to complete the inside of the cards with the words. Remind them to look for rhyming words.

> **Answers**
> 1 lives   2 starts   3 well   4 tears

4 Ask learners to complete the card using the writing frame.

Extension
Ask learners to find three other kinds of card in a card shop and report back to the class.

Answers: Self-study exercises

A card for you

Your own notes

1 2 congratulations   3 wedding

2 1 For a special mum
   2 Congratulations on your new baby
   3 With love on your birthday

A card for you 16c

1 Complete the front of the cards. Use these words.

| Happy wedding day   Congratulations on your new baby   For a special mum |

1

2

3

2 Match the words with the same sounds.

1 tears a tell
2 well   b years
3 start   c lives
4 eyes   d heart

3 Complete the cards. Use these words.

| lives   starts   tears   well |

A

First in your eyes,
First in your
(1) .... ,
First in your hearts, as a new
life (2) ....

B

A Mother's Day wish to say
we love you more than words
can tell –
Not just on Mother's Day,
but every other day as
(3) ....

C

Wishing you a life full of
happy years,
Always laughter, never
(4) ....

4 Write a Thank you card.

Dear .... ,
I just wanted to say

| many thanks
thanks a lot
thank you so much | for | everything.
all you do.
all your help. | You're really | helpful.
kind.
understanding. | |
| | | | You're a | special
great
wonderful | person. |

Yours,

....

Self-study exercises

1a How do you spell that?

1 Make sentences.

1 name what's your   *What's your name?*
2 spell you Jack how do   ....
3 that spell how you do   ....

2 Complete.

a .*A*.   b .*B*.   c ....   d ....   e ....   f ....   g ....   h ....   i ....   j ....   k ....   l ....   m ....
n ....   o ....   p ....   q ....   r ....   s ....   t ....   u ....   v ....   w ....   x ....   y ....   z ....

3 Complete.

A: Hello, (1) ....*my*........ name (2) .... Hussein.
B: Sorry, (3) .... do you (4) .... Hussein?
A: (5) H-U- ....

1b Timetables

1 Complete.

1 ....*Monday*...   3 ....   5 ....   7 ....
2 ....   4 ....   6 ....

2 Order the questions.

1 Tuesday is maths on   *Is maths on Tuesday?*
2 is morning on listening Monday   ....
3 Wednesday speaking where's on   ....
4 morning Wednesday on what's   ....

1c Personal details

1 Write the questions.

1 you are old how   *How old are you?*
2 name what's your   ....
3 do live where you   ....
4 student number what's your   ....

2 Match the questions in 1 with the answers.

a I'm 20 years old. ....*1*....
b In London.   ....
c ML 63   ....
d My name is Wei. ....

3 Write about Alex.

Name: Alex West
Age: 45
City: Leeds
Student number: UB 63

His name is ...

2a Where are you from?

1 Complete the table.

country	nationality	language
Turkey	Turkish	
		Chinese
Iraq		

2 Complete the questions.

1 .....*Where*..... are you from?
2 What's your capital .... ?
3 What's .... nationality?

4 .... your home town?
5 What .... do you speak?

3 Write about you.

My name is .... I am from .... – the capital city is .... Now I live in
.... I am .... years old. I speak .... and a little ....

2b I live in a flat

1 Order the letters and make words.

1 ftal ....   2 ubs psto ....   3 kpra ....   4 oloshc ....

2 Complete.

1 I live ....*in*.... Glasgow .... a block of flats.
2 My house is .... London Road.
3 The bus stop is .... the railway station.
4 Our college is .... Whitworth Street.
5 My friend lives .... St Anne's Street, ... the park.

3 Read and answer.

1 How old is Sevda? .*She's 18 years old.*..........
2 Where's Sevda from?
....
3 Where does she live?
....

4 Who does she live with?
....
5 What does she live next to?
....

> I'm Sevda, I'm 18 years old and I'm from Iraq. I live in a flat with my mother and father.
> We live on Princess Road, next to the park.

2c New home

1 Correct the addresses.

N parha ..*N Parha*..............
lady margaret road 121 ....
southall ....
Middlesex ....
UBI 2nw ....

LI Ho ....
FLAT 2 ....
13 edgemont Street ....
Shawlands ....
Glasgow ....
g4l 3eh ....

2 Write the opposites.

1 noisy ......*quiet*......
2 friendly ....

3 horrible ....
4 dirty ....

3a Can you say that again?

1 Complete the sentences with these words.

| open   put   turn |

1 .... your books.
2 .... over to the next page.

3 .... your file on the desk.

2 Complete the sentences.

1 ....*Can*....... you say that again?
2 .... me, which page is it?
3 What does *projector* .... ?
4 Bekele: How do you .... *handout*?   Rachel: H-A-N-D-O-U-T.

3 Complete the conversation.

| ~~excuse me~~   thank you   of course   I'm sorry |

Muhammad: (1) ..*Excuse me*.. , can you give me a pen?
    Irshad: (2) .... , can you say that again?
Muhammad: Yes, can you give me a pen?
    Irshad: Yes, (3) .... Here you are.
Muhammad: (4) .... very much.

3b Class rules

1 Make negative sentences.

1 Smoke in class.   *Don't smoke in class.*........................
2 Put your litter on the floor.   ....
3 Be late for class.   ....
4 Do another student's homework.   ....
5 Speak your language in class – speak English.   ....

2 Read and tick (✓) or cross (✗).

1 Students eat in the library. ....*X*....
2 Students study in the library. ....
3 In the library, students listen to music. ....
4 Students can chat there. ....
5 In the library, students use their mobile phones. ....

Library rules

Welcome to the library.
You can study or you can take books home. Don't bring any food or drinks. Turn off your mobile phones. Do not listen to music or chat. Smoking is not allowed.

3c A note to college

1 Correct the spelling.

1 attendence ..*attendance*..
2 leter ....

3 posible ....
4 problem ....

5 offis ....

2 Complete the phrases.

| ~~possible~~   soon   sorry   would like |

1 Is it ....*possible*....to get a letter from you?
2 I .... some help with my homework.

3 I'm .... I'm late.
4 Can I see you as .... as possible?

3 Order the words.

Dear _____ ,
sorry I'm. ....*I'm sorry*...
can't I come to class your. ....
ill feel I. ....
Yours, Satar

From *ESOL Activities Entry 1* © Cambridge University Press 2008   **PHOTOCOPIABLE**

4a Time

1 Write.

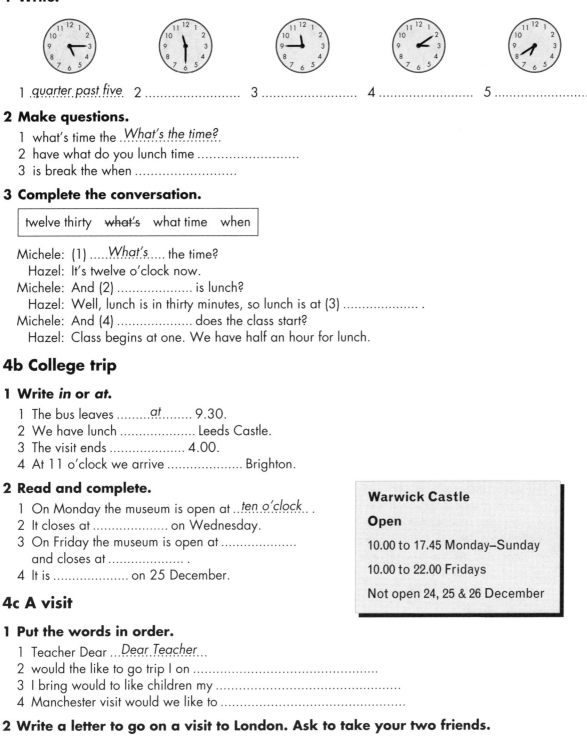

1 *quarter past five* 2 .... 3 .... 4 .... 5 ....

2 Make questions.

1 what's time the ....*What's the time?*....
2 have what do you lunch time ....
3 is break the when ....

3 Complete the conversation.

| twelve thirty | ~~what's~~ | what time | when |

Michele: (1) .....*What's*..... the time?
  Hazel: It's twelve o'clock now.
Michele: And (2) .... is lunch?
  Hazel: Well, lunch is in thirty minutes, so lunch is at (3) ....
Michele: And (4) .... does the class start?
  Hazel: Class begins at one. We have half an hour for lunch.

4b College trip

1 Write *in* or *at*.

1 The bus leaves ....*at*........ 9.30.
2 We have lunch .... Leeds Castle.
3 The visit ends .... 4.00.
4 At 11 o'clock we arrive .... Brighton.

2 Read and complete.

1 On Monday the museum is open at ..*ten o'clock*.. .
2 It closes at .... on Wednesday.
3 On Friday the museum is open at ....
   and closes at ....
4 It is .... on 25 December.

> **Warwick Castle**
>
> **Open**
>
> 10.00 to 17.45 Monday–Sunday
>
> 10.00 to 22.00 Fridays
>
> Not open 24, 25 & 26 December

4c A visit

1 Put the words in order.

1 Teacher Dear ...*Dear Teacher*...
2 would the like to go trip I on ....
3 I bring would to like children my ....
4 Manchester visit would we like to ....

2 Write a letter to go on a visit to London. Ask to take your two friends.

(date) ....

Dear ....

....
....
....
....

Yours,

....

5a Morning

1 Complete.

| brush | drink | get | close | have | make | say | ~~wake up~~ |

In the morning I (1) ...*wake up*... early and (2) .... out of bed. I (3) .... a shower and (4) .... my teeth. Then I (5) .... breakfast and (6) .... my tea. I (7) .... goodbye to my family at eight o'clock and (8) .... the door.

2 Write three sentences about your morning.

....
....
....

5b My family

1 Match.

| his | ~~my~~ | her | our | their | its | your |

1 I – ....*my*........   5 it – ....
2 you – ....   6 we – ....
3 he – ....   7 they – ....
4 she – ....

2 Read and complete.

There are five people in my family. My name is Hannah and I've got one brother and one sister. My brother's name is Karl and my sister's name is Barbara. My mother's name is Jane and her husband (my father) is called David.

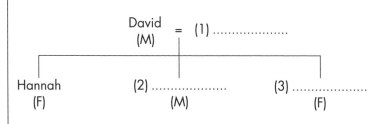

5c Julia's day

1 Write.

1 ...*wash up*... 2 .... 3 .... 4 .... 5 .... 6 .... 7 ....

2 Complete.

Taghrid wakes up at seven o'clock and makes breakfast. She (1) ...*washes up*... and

 (2) .... She meets her friend and (3) .... to college with her.

They have lunch at 12.30. In the afternoon Taghrid 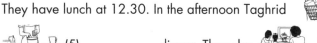 (4) .... In the evening she

 (5) .... dinner. Then she (5) .... TV.

6a At the market

1 Put the questions in order.

1 much how peppers are the   ...*How much are the peppers?*...
2 bananas do have you any   ....
3 that much is how   ....

2 Complete the conversation.

altogether	~~get~~	here	how much	OK	want

Seller: Hello, what can I (1) ....*get*....... you today?
Jolanta: Let me think. I (2) .... a kilo of tomatoes.
Seller: OK, (3) .... you are.
Jolanta: And two peppers.
Seller: (4) ....
Jolanta: Thanks. (5) .... is that?
Seller: It's one pound thirty-five (6) ....

6b Going shopping

1 Label the plan.

| car park |
| cinema |
| restaurants |
| shops |

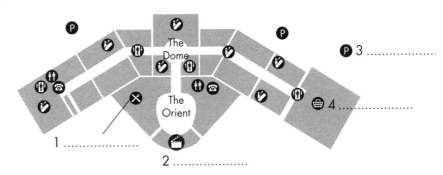

1 ....
2 ....
P 3 ....
4 ....

2 Write the numbers.

1 36 ....*thirty-six*....
2 230 ....
3 10,000 ....
4 30,000,000 ....

3 Complete with numbers from exercise 2.

The Trafford Centre has (1) ...*two hundred and thirty* shops. There are (2) ....
restaurants and (3) .... car parking spaces. (4) .... visitors go there
every year.

6c A shopping list

1 Write.

1 .*a jar of*... jam   2 .... chocolates   3 .... sugar   4 .... milk

2 Read the notes and write the list.

Ali,
Don't forget to buy
a bag of sugar and
a bottle of milk for
tonight.
Zohra

Ali,
When you go to the shops,
remember to buy a jar
of coffee, two bottles of
cola and four packets of
crisps.
Thanks,
Marta

Shopping list
1 *a bag of sugar*..............
2 ....
3 ....
4 ....
5 ....

7a Welcome

1 Write sentences.

1 up we kitchen in wash the .... *We wash up in the kitchen.* ....
2 have we a in the bathroom shower ....
3 we eat dinner in room the dining ....
4 watch we in living the room TV ....

2 Complete the conversation.

> ~~come in~~   really nice   show you around   upstairs   what a lovely house

Gregor: Peter, (1) .... *come in* .... . How are you?
  Peter: I'm fine. (2) .... !
Gregor: Let me (3) .... The living room is here and the kitchen is next door.
  Peter: How many bedrooms are there?
Gregor: (4) .... there are two bedrooms and a bathroom.
  Peter: It's (5) ....
Gregor: Thank you.

7b A flat to rent

1 Order the letters and make words.

Rooms:
1 ikcetnh ..... *kitchen* .....
2 bodroem ....
3 ivlign ormo ....

4 lhal ....
5 atrobomh ....

2 Order the letters and make words.

Furniture:
1 iksn .... *sink* ....
2 fosa ....
3 tbah ....

4   tairdaro ....
5   arderwob ....

3 Write.

> opposite   ~~under~~   in the middle of   next to

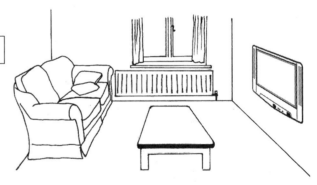

The radiator is (1) ...... *under* ...... the window. The sofa is (2) .... the radiator. The TV is (3) .... the sofa. The coffee table is (4) .... the room.

7c My room

1 Write the words.

1 .... *quilt* ....   2 ....   3 ....   4 ....

2 Complete with on, under or in.

1 My books are .... *on* .... the shelves.
2 My shoes are .... the bed.

3 My jacket is .... the back of the door.
4 My clothes are .... the wardrobe.

8a Sports, hobbies and interests

1 Put into groups.

chess dancing football shopping ~~swimming~~ tennis

go: ...*swimming*... , ... , ...
play: .... , ... , ...

2 Complete the conversation.

Timmi: Hi, Khaled, do you want to (1) ....*play*.......tennis this afternoon?
Khaled: I'm sorry, Timmi, I (2) .... play tennis.
Timmi: Well, do you want to (3) .... football tomorrow?
Khaled: Yes, OK, I (4) .... play football very (5) ....

8b Sports rules

1 Label the pictures.

behind   in front of   over

1 .... 2 .... 3 ....

2 Write.

   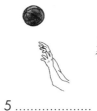 

1 ....*head*.... 2 .... 3 .... 4 .... 5 .... 6 ....

3 Write sentences.

In a football game …
1 kick the ball ✓   *In a football game you can kick the ball.*
2 head the ball ✓   ....
3 catch the ball ✗   ....
4 kick another player ✗   ....
5 score a goal ✓   ....

8c Our sports centre

1 Write

1 ....*aerobics*.... 2 .... 3 .... 4 .... 5 ....

2 Make sentences.

1 Josh play tennis (✓) + play badminton (✓)   *Josh can play tennis and he can play badminton.*
2 Silvie do yoga (✓) × do weight training (✗)   *Silvie can do yoga but she can't do weight training.*
3 Ahmed play football (✓) × play tennis (✗)   ....
4 Mia swim (✗) × do aerobics (✓)   ....
5 Khaled play table tennis (✓) + play basketball (✓)   ....
6 Latifa go running (✗) × do yoga (✓)   ....

9a A single to Oxford Street

1 Write the names of the tickets.

1 all day travel on any bus or train ....
2 one journey ....
3 for journey back on the same route ....

2 Complete.

Julian: (1) ..... _I'd like_ ..... a ticket to the city centre.
Bus driver: (2) .... are you going in the city centre?
Julian: I'm going to Prince Street.
Bus driver: Do you want a (3) .... or a (4) .... ?
Julian: I'm going back to Clifton, so I'd like a return, please.
Bus driver: (5) .... one pound fifty, please.

9b Travel pass

1 Complete.

anyone anything ~~any time~~ anywhere

1 When do you want to leave? We can go ... _any time_ ....
2 They can travel where they like. They can travel ....
3 I don't have any money, I don't have ....
4 Do you know the other students? No, I don't know .... here.

2 Read and answer.

Young Person's Railcard

Just one trip and the card could pay for itself. Anyone between 16 and 25 can buy a Young Person's Railcard for just £20. It saves you 1/3 on many rail fares in Great Britain for a whole year.

1 Who can buy a Young Person's Railcard? _Anyone between 16 and 25._ ....
2 How much is it? ....
3 How long can you use it for? ....

9c Travelling

1 Complete with *expensive, comfortable, quick, cheap.*

1 Travelling by taxi is ... _expensive_ ... .
2 I prefer to go by train because it is ....
3 We go to town by car because it is ....
4 The bus to the city is not expensive, it's ....

2 Write.

When I visit my friend, I (1) .... travelling by (2) .... because it is
(3) .... But when I visit my friend in Edinburgh, my (4) .... way of travelling
(5) .... train because it is a long way and the train is (6) ....

10a Can you tell me the way to the bus station?

1 Order the letters to make words.

1 ubs post ....*bus stop*....
2 rac aprk ....
3 abezr nroscsig ....
4 fractfi lgisht ....

2 Write.

1 .... 2 .... 3 ....

3 Complete the conversation.

Leyla: Excuse me, (1) ....*can you*.... tell me the way to the bank?
Woman: Yes, of course. Now, from the train station here, you (2) .... left and go
(3) .... down the High Street.
Leyla: I see.
Woman: When you come to the zebra crossing, the bank is on (4) .... left.

10b Visitors' day

1 Write questions.

1 far is how the town hall .*How far is the town hall?*
2 how get does it long take to to the college ....
3 how many is it the bus metres stop to ....

2 Read and choose A, B, C or D.

Department Open Day

Programme
9.15 Welcome
9.30 Tour

How to find us
From the railway station, turn left and go up
the High Street for 500 metres. Turn right down
Main Road and go straight on for one kilometre.
At the traffic lights, go straight on again and
take the next left. After about five minutes'
walk, the college is on the right.

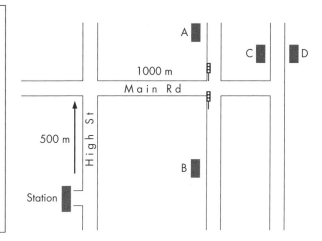

10c Where's the party?

1 Write in full.

1 Rd .... 2 St .... 3 La ....

2 Complete.

~~are having~~ at celebrate party

Andrea

We (1) ..*are having*... a party. Come and (2) ....
with us. The (3) .... is on Saturday
(4) .... 4.

Ceyhan

11a What's my job?

1 Match the jobs with the places.

1 cook   A office
2 nurse   B taxi
3 taxi driver   C hospital
4 secretary   D kitchen

2 Write questions.

1 do outside work inside or you ..*Do you work inside or outside?*..
2 machines you work with do people or ....
3 in you work a big do place ....
4 you do factory work in a ....

11b Person wanted

1 Write.

1 ph ...*per hour*...
2 P/T ....
3 IT ....
4 Mon ....
5 K ....

2 Complete the sentences.

1 Cook needed for busy restaurant.   We ......*need*...... a cook for our restaurant.
2 Good teachers wanted for college.   We .... a good teacher for our college.
3 Secretary wanted for city centre office.   We .... a secretary for our city centre office.
4 Taxi driver needed next week.   We .... a taxi driver for next week.

3 Read and answer.

Driver wanted

P/T driver needed to help old people go to shops.
2 hrs a day, Thurs – Sat am. Tel: 0208 754 2316.

1 What is the job? ......*Driver*......
2 Is the job full-time or part-time? ....
3 How many hours is it? ....
4 What days is the job? ....

11c A job application

1 Match the opposites.

1 hard-working   A lazy
2 polite   B disorganised
3 organised   C rude

2 Complete.

Dear Sir,

I would like (1) ....*to apply*.... for the job of waiter
in your restaurant. I am (2) .... and
(3) .... I am (4) .... to work
at the weekend and in the (5) ....
(6) .... ,

Jothy Pushpa

12a Would you like a drink?

1 Write in full.

1 White tea with two sugars.
cup / tea / milk / two spoons / sugar .... *A cup of tea with milk and two spoons of sugar.* ....
2 White coffee, one sugar.
cup / coffee / milk / one spoon / sugar ....
3 Black tea, two sugars.
cup / tea / no milk / two spoons / sugar ....

2 Write.

| like   don't like   love |

hate   1 ....   2 ....   3 ....

3 Put into groups.

Can I get a coffee?   Can I get you anything?   Can I have a biscuit?   ~~Could I have a cup of tea?~~
What can I get you?   Would you like something to eat?

1 asking for something: *Could I have a cup of tea?* ....
2 offering something: ....

12b A menu

1 Write.

1 yatst ...... *tasty* ......   2 volley ....   3 sedliciou ....

2 Read and answer.

Attention all visitors!

Feeling hungry? Would you like something to eat? Then why not call into our restaurant on the first floor? Our opening times are:

BREAKFAST   7.45 am – 10.45 am Monday to Friday
8.15 am – 10.30 am Saturday and Sunday
LUNCH   11.45 – 1.15
EVENING   4.45 – 7.15

Come in and enjoy the food.

1 Where is the restaurant?
on the first floor ....
2 What can you get in the restaurant?
....
3 When is breakfast on Sunday?
....
4 What time is the evening meal?
....

12c A recipe

1 Make words.

1 ourp ...... *pour* ......   3 xmi ....   5 akerb ....
2 dad ....   4 thea ....   6 eltm ....

2 Write C (countable) or U (uncountable).

1 butter .. *U* .   2 tomatoes .....   3 sugar .....   4 onions .....   5 salt .....   6 eggs .....

3 Complete the recipe with these words.

| add   cook   heat   mix   put |

Rice pudding

(1) ...... *Put* ...... 50 grams of rice and half a litre of milk into a pan and (2) .... it. Turn down the heat and (3) .... for 30 minutes. (4) .... in 25 grams of sugar with 25 grams of butter and (5) .... until the sugar and butter melt. Serve immediately.

13a The weather

1 Write the adjectives.

1 rain – ......*rainy*......   3 wind – ....   5 storm – ....

2 sun – ....   4 ice – ....

2 Complete.

| cold   dear   don't worry   ~~like~~   raincoat |

Monika: What's the weather (1) ....*like*....... outside?

Ali: It's (2) .... and it's raining.

Monika: Oh (3) .... I haven't got my (4) ....

Ali: (5) .... , you can have my umbrella.

13b Great British weather

1 Complete.

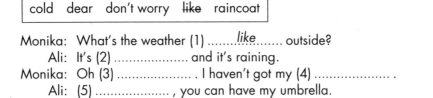

1 ....

4 ....

2 ....

3 ....

2 Complete.

| cool   mild   warm |

hot   1 ....   2 ....   3 ....   cold

3 Read and answer.

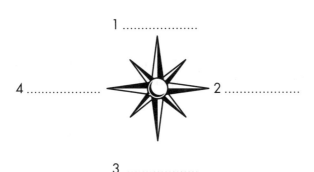

Today is dry with sunshine, but some cloud is coming in. Scotland starts cloudy but becomes sunny in the afternoon. Generally, today is warm, but wind from the south-west is keeping the temperature cool.

1 What is the weather like in most places?

....

2 What is the weather like in Scotland in the morning?

....

3 What is keeping the temperature cool?

....

13c Clothes

1 Write in order.

1 wool a black hat   *a black wool hat.*.............................

2 leather shoes comfortable   ....

3 slippers old red   ....

4 fashionable blue hoodie a   ....

2 Complete with *a pair of* or – .

1 ...*a pair of*... shoes   2 .... hats   3 .... shorts

4 .... trousers   5 .... jumpers   6 .... scarves

14a At the doctor's

1 Write.

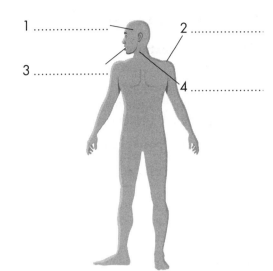

1 .....*head*...... 3 ....
2 .... 4 ....

2 Make words.

| ~~back~~ head stomach throat |

1 ..*back*.. ache   3 .... ache
2 .... ache   4 sore ....

3 Complete.

Doctor Watson: What's the (1) .....*matter*...... ?
Janos: I've got a (2) .... throat.
Doctor Watson: (3) .... me see. Are you taking (4) .... for this?
Janos: Yes, I'm drinking hot lemon.
Doctor Watson: Well, here's a (5) .... for some medicine too.

14b Medicine labels

1 Make words.

1 balett ......*tablet*......   3 aremc ....   5 iemdncie ....
2 csaulep ....   4 dpweor ....

2 Read and answer.

1 What is the medicine for?
2 Can a 10-year-old child take this?
3 How many tablets can you take in 24 hours?

Recommended for		
Coughs	Colds	Sore throat

Directions
Swallow the tablet with a glass of water

Age	Dosage
Adults, Children over 12	2 tablets 3 times a day
Children under 12	Not recommended

⚠ WARNING.
No more than 6 capsules
in 24 hours

Not for children under 12.

14c An absence note

1 Order the words.

1 me excuse please *Please excuse me.*   3 soon get well ....
2 come I'm I sorry but can't ....

2 Complete the sentences.

Dear Miss Jones,

Please excuse me, but we (1) ..*are not feeling*.. (not feeling) very well
today. My wife (2) .... (take care) of my daughter today. I
have a bad cold. At the moment I (3) .... (lie) in bed. I
(4) .... (read) a book, but I (5) .... (not enjoy) myself.

Ahmed

15a Sending a parcel

1 Order the questions.

1 all is that   *Is that all?* ....

2 you what I do can for   ....

3 you put could it on scales the   ....

4 you got stamp a second-class have   ....

2 Complete the conversation with these words.

all   envelope   second-class   stamp

Customer: Can I have a (1) .... , please?

     Clerk: Here you are. Is that (2) .... ?

Customer: Have you got an (3) .... too?

15b Special Delivery

1 Write the words.

1 ....*receive*....   2 ....   3 ....   4 ....

2 Look at the pictures and order the sentences.

1   2   3   4

A Now put the letter in the post box.   ....

B Then decide on first- or second-class post.   ....

C First put the letter on the scales.   ....

D After that put the stamp on the letter.   ....

15c Thank you

1 Order the letters to make words.

1 doog ......*good*......   3 trgae ....

2 olvley ....   4 cien ....

2 Complete the sentences with *lovely*, *great* or *nice*.

1 What .....*lovely*..... flowers!

2 That's a .... dress.

3 It's a .... film.

4 What a .... present!

3 Complete the note.

Dear .... ,

What a great .... ! Thanks for .... me.

Here's a .... for you. Hope you ....

Kim

16a After you

1 Complete with *me* or *you*.

1 Excuse ....*me*........   2 After ....   3 Pardon ....   4 Thank ....

2 Order the questions.

1 queue is the end of this the ..*Is this the end of the queue?*..
2 free seat this is ....
3 like sit to here you would ....
4 is seat this free ....

3 Complete the conversation.

| anyway | free | free | me | ~~pardon~~ | sorry | thanks |

Isabel: (1) .....*Pardon*..... me, is this seat (2) .... ?
  Will: I'm (3) .... , but someone is sitting here.
Isabel: OK, thanks (4) .... Pardon (5) .... , is anyone sitting here?
Carol: No, it's (6) ....
Isabel: Oh, (7) .... very much.

16b Good manners

1 Write sentences.

1 *She's knocking on the door.*   2 ....   3 ....   4 ....

2 Read and find five times when we say sorry.

People in the UK say sorry a lot. But when do we say sorry? We say sorry when we can't speak to someone (*Sorry, I don't have time to talk now.*) or when someone does something bad (*Sorry, my son is always breaking things.*). We say sorry when we don't hear something (*Sorry, can you say that again?*) or when we want someone to tell us something again (*Sorry, I'm not sure what you mean.*). Finally, we say sorry when we feel sorry (*I'm sorry.*).

1 *We say sorry when we can't speak to someone.*
2 ....
3 ....
4 ....
5 ....

16c A card for you

1 Write.

1 csepali   .....*special*.....
2 gonsrctiatulaon   ....
3 degwndi   ....

2 Order.

1 a mum for special   ....
2 your congratulations baby on new   ....
3 love on with birthday your ....

Audioscript

1a How do you spell that?
Track 2
Hello, I'm Jessica. That's J-E-S-S-I-C-A.
Hi, my name's David. That's D-A-V-I-D.
I'm Butri. That's B-U-T-R-I.
Hello, I'm Megan. That's M-E-G-A-N.
Hi, I'm Thomas. That's T-H-O-M-A-S.
My name's Zakir. That's Z-A-K-I-R.

Track 3
a h j k   b c d e g p t v   i y   o
q u w   f l m n s x z   r

Track 4
1 I'm Ahmed. That's capital A-H-M-E-D.
2 My name's Charlotte. That's capital C-H-A-R-L-O-double-T-E.
3 Hello, I'm called Joseph. That's J-O-S-E-P-H.

Track 5
1
David: What's your name?
Butri: I'm Butri. That's B-U-T-R-I.

2
Thomas: Hello, my name's Thomas.
Butri: Sorry. How do you spell Thomas?
Thomas: T-H-O-M-A-S.

3
Zakir: I'm Zakir.
Megan: Sorry. How do you spell that?
Zakir: Z-A-K-I-R.

1b Timetables
Track 6
1 Monday   2 Tuesday   3 Wednesday
4 Thursday   5 Friday   6 Saturday   7 Sunday

2a Where are you from?
Track 7
Scotland   Ireland   Poland   Sudan   Iran   Iraq

Track 8
1
Hasan: Hi, my name's Hasan.
Maria: Hello, Hasan. Where are you from?
Hasan: I'm from Sudan. I'm Sudanese but I live in Germany.
Maria: Oh, really? Do you speak German?
Hasan: Yes, I do. But my first language is Arabic.

2
Joanna: Bangon, you're from Thailand, aren't you?
Bangon: Yes, I am. I'm Thai – my home town is Chiang Mai. Where are you from, Joanna?
Joanna: Me? I'm from Poland. I'm Polish.

3
Daniel: Are you from Rome or Naples, Marco?
Marco: I'm from Rome. What about you, Daniel? Where are you from?
Daniel: I'm from Bucharest in Romania.
Marco: What language do you speak in Romania?
Daniel: We speak Romanian. Listen. *Ceau* – that means 'hello'.
Marco: Oh really? *Ciao* mean 'hello' in Italian too.

Track 9
1 Where are you from?
2 What's your capital city?
3 What's your nationality?
4 What's your home town?
5 What languages do you speak?

3a Can you say that again?
Track 10
1
Rachel: OK, everyone – it's time to start. Open your books at Unit 3, please.
Hamad: Excuse me, Rachel, can you say that again, please?
Rachel: Yes, of course. Turn to Unit 3, activity 1.

2
Tharntip: I'm sorry, Rachel.
Rachel: Yes, what is it, Tharntip?
Tharntip: How do you spell *computer*?
Rachel: C-O-M-P-U-T-E-R.

3
Rachel: OK, that's all for today then. Put your handouts in your file for the next class.
Andras: I'm sorry, I don't understand. What does *handout* mean?
Rachel: A handout is the piece of paper I give you.

Track 11
Can you say that again, please?
How do you spell *computer*?
I don't understand.
What does *handout* mean?

4a Time
Track 12
1 It's ten past three.
2 The time is quarter to eight.
3 It's twenty-five past two.
4 The time now is twenty to six.
5 It's five to five.

Track 13

Anna: Hi, Khaled.

Khaled: Hello, Anna.

Anna: Can I ask you some questions?

Khaled: Sure.

Anna: OK – first question. What time do you have breakfast?

Khaled: We eat breakfast at about seven o'clock in the morning.

Anna: So that's seven o'clock. And when is lunch?

Khaled: I have lunch at half past twelve.

Anna: Five past twelve.

Khaled: No, no. I have lunch at half past twelve – twelve thirty.

Anna: Sorry, so you have lunch at half past twelve. OK. And what time do you have dinner?

Khaled: I have dinner at quarter past six.

Anna: So that's six fifteen. Thank you, Khaled.

Track 14

What time do you have breakfast?

When is lunch?

5a Morning
Track 15

It's seven o'clock in the morning. Wake up … and get out of bed … Wash your face … Now brush your teeth … Have a shower … Make breakfast … and drink your tea … Say goodbye to everyone … Goodbye! Bye! … and close the door.

Track 16

Interviewer: Excuse me, can I ask you some questions?

Ala: What about?

Interviewer: It's about your morning.

Ala: Yes, OK. Why not?

Interviewer: First of all, what's your name?

Ala: I'm Ala.

Interviewer: Do you wake up early?

Ala: Yes, I do. I wake up at six thirty.

Interviewer: Do you have a shower in the morning?

Ala: Yes, I do. I have a shower in the morning.

Interviewer: Who makes breakfast? Do you make breakfast?

Ala: Yes, I do. I make breakfast.

Interviewer: Do you get the children ready?

Ala: Yes, I do. I brush their teeth and wash their faces and then I dress them.

Interviewer: Do you go to college?

Ala: Yes, in the morning I study English.

Interviewer: Do you do your homework in the morning?

Ala: No, I don't. I do my homework in the evening.

Track 17

1 Do you wake up early?
2 Do you have a shower in the morning?
3 Do you make breakfast?
4 Do you get the children ready?
5 Do you go to college?
6 Do you do your homework in the morning?

Track 18

Do you make breakfast?

Yes, I do.

Do you do your homework in the morning?

No, I don't.

5c Julia's day
Track 19

Julia wakes up at seven o'clock. She makes breakfast and takes the children to school. She makes the beds, washes up and tidies up. At ten o'clock Julia walks to the town centre, does the shopping and carries the bags home. She meets her friend for lunch. In the afternoon she cleans and does the washing. Then she cooks dinner. In the evening Julia plays with her children and talks to her husband, and then she watches TV.

6a At the market
Track 20

22p   40p   65p   93p   50p   45p
37p   32p   £1.10   £1.30

Track 21

Seller: Hello, love, what can I get you today?

Jolanta: Let me think. I want two kilos of potatoes.

Seller: Two kilos of potatoes. Here you are.

Jolanta: And a kilo of tomatoes.

Seller: OK.

Jolanta: And one and a half kilos of onions.

Seller: Here you are.

Jolanta: Thanks. How much is that?

Seller: Two pounds sixteen altogether, please.

6b Going shopping
Track 22

one hundred
two hundred and thirty
ten thousand
thirty million

7a Welcome
Track 23
kitchen   We cook meals in the kitchen.
dining room   We eat in the dining room.
hall   We keep our coats in the hall.
bathroom   We have a shower in the bathroom.
living room   We relax in the living room.
bedroom   We sleep in the bedroom.
living room   We watch TV in the living room.

Track 24
Julia: Hello, Jemma. Come in.
Jemma: Thanks, Julia.
Julia: Let me show you around. The living room is here on the left.
Jemma: What a nice room!
Julia: The kitchen is next to the living room. Upstairs there are two bedrooms and a bathroom.
Jemma: What a lovely house! It's a really nice place.
Julia: Thank you.

Track 25
Come in.
Let me show you around.
What a lovely house!
It's a really nice place.

7c My room
Track 26
My room is very small. In my room I have a lot of stuff. My bed is next to the window. It's a single bed. I have a lot of things under the bed, like my bag and some shoes. I have two pillows and a quilt on my bed. There are some shelves opposite my bed with books and CDs on them. There is a cupboard next to the door. My cupboard is full of clothes, and I have my jewellery and pens on top of the cupboard. I keep my jacket on the back of the door. I'm not very tidy.

8a Sports, hobbies and interests
Track 27
1
Tom: Do you want to go swimming, Daniel?
Daniel: No, I'm sorry, I can't swim.
Tom: Oh dear.

2
John: Jessica, can you play cards?
Jessica: Yes, I can. I can play lots of card games.
John: How about a game now?
Jessica: I'm sorry, I can't. I'm busy.

3
Ben: This is a great song – come on, Pranee, let's dance.
Pranee: Oh, Ben – you know I can't dance.
Ben: Of course you can – everyone can dance. I'm a great dancer – I can dance very well. Come on!

4
Ewa: Do you play any musical instruments, Mia?
Mia: What do you mean?
Ewa: For example, the guitar, the piano, the violin?
Mia: Oh yes, I can play the guitar. What can you play, Ewa?
Ewa: I can play the guitar too. Would you like to play together?
Mia: Yes, sure.

Track 28
I can play the guitar.
I can dance very well.
I can't swim.
I can't dance.

9a A single to Oxford Street
Track 29
1
Passenger 1: I'd like a ticket to the city centre, please.
Bus driver: Where are you going?
Passenger 1: Oxford Street.
Bus driver: Is that a single or return?
Passenger 1: Return, please.
Bus driver: That's four pounds, please.
Passenger 1: Thanks.

2
Passenger 2: Are you going to Battersea Park Road?
Bus driver: Yes.
Passenger 2: OK. Let's get on.
Passenger 3: Two tickets to South Thames College, please.
Bus driver: Are those singles, returns, or have you got Travelcards?
Passenger 3: Singles, please.
Bus driver: Four pounds, please.
Passenger 3: There you are.

3
Passenger 4: Hi, we're going to Hyde Park.
Passenger 5: And then we'd like to go to the city centre.
Bus driver: Do you have Travelcards?
Passenger 4: Yes, we do – here they are.
Bus driver: OK.
Passenger 4: Can you tell us when to get off?
Bus driver: Sure, just sit over there.

Track 30
I'd like a ticket to the city centre, please.
Two tickets to South Thames College, please.
Hi, we're going to Hyde Park.
Can you tell us when to get off?

10a Can you tell me the way to the bus station?
Track 31

1

Sergei: Excuse me, can you tell me the way to the bus station?

Man: OK, we are here, at the school.

Sergei: Yes.

Man: Go down the High Street.

Sergei: OK.

Man: Go across Market Street and Park Road.

Sergei: Yes.

Man: Turn right at the bus stop and go down Railway Street.

Sergei: OK.

Man: The bus station is on your right, on Railway Street.

Sergei: Ah! Thank you.

2

Nongluck: Excuse me. How can I get to the supermarket?

Woman: From the car park, turn left and go down Park Road.

Nongluck: OK.

Woman: When you get to the traffic lights, turn right.

Nongluck: Yes.

Woman: Then go straight on.

Nongluck: I see.

Woman: Go across the road at the zebra crossing, and the supermarket is opposite the school.

Nongluck: Thank you very much.

Track 32

Can you tell me the way to the bus station?

How can I get to the supermarket?

11a What's my job?
Track 33

A: OK, let's play *What's my job?* I'll start. You ask me ten questions and try to guess my job. I can only answer with *yes* or *no*.

B: OK. So, do you work inside?

A: Yes, I do. I work inside a lot of the time.

B: OK. Do you work with your hands?

A: Yes and no. I think I work with my hands a lot, but I sometimes work at a desk.

B: Do you work with people?

A: Yes, I do, I work with people, but I also use machines.

B: This is difficult. Do you work in a small place?

A: No, I don't. I work in a big place.

B: Do you like your job?

A: Yes, I do. I like it a lot.

B: Do you get a lot of money for your work?

A: No, not really.

B: Do you work in a factory?

A: No, I don't. I don't work in a factory.

B: Do you work in a hospital?

A: Yes, I do, I work in a hospital.

B: Are you a doctor?

A: No, sorry, I'm not a doctor. I win!

B: Oh. OK, my turn now. Let me think. Right, I'm ready.

A: OK. Do you work with your hands?

B: Yes, I do.

A: Do you work with people or with machines?

B: That's two questions.

A: OK. Do you work with people?

B: Yes, I work with a group of people.

A: Do you work with machines?

B: Yes, I work with machines too.

A: Do you work inside?

B: No, I work outside.

A: So you work outside, with your hands, with a group of people and with machines.

B: That's correct.

A: Do you build houses?

B: Yes.

A: Then I think you're a builder.

B: You're right.

Track 34

Do you work in a hospital?   Yes, I do.

Do you work in a factory?   No, I don't.

Do you get a lot of money?   No, not really.

Do you like your job?   Yes, I do.

Do you work with your hands?   Yes and no.

12a Would you like a drink?
Track 35

1

Jessica: Hi, Jolanta. Hello, Nongluck. Come in.

Nongluck: Thanks.

Jessica: Can I get you anything? Would you like a drink?

Nongluck: I'd love a glass of water.

Jessica: And for you, Jolanta?

Jolanta: Could I have a cup of tea?

Jessica: Yes, of course. How do you like it?

Jolanta: White with two sugars, please.

Jessica: Would you like something to eat? Can I get you a biscuit?

Jolanta: No, thanks.

Jessica: How about you, Nongluck? What can I get you?

Nongluck: I'd like a biscuit, please. I love sweet things.

2
Assistant: Good morning.
Anita: Hi, can I get a black coffee, please?
Assistant: Sure, just one minute. And can I get you anything else? A cake?
Anita: No thanks, I don't really like cakes.
Assistant: And for you?
Muhammad: Well, I like cakes a lot, but just a coffee for me too. Thanks, anyway.

Track 36
Can I get you anything?
Could I have a cup of tea?
Would you like something to eat?
What can I get you?
Can I get you anything else?

12c A recipe
Track 37
Now today I'm going to make the perfect omelette, and for this we'll need two or three fresh eggs, milk, salt and pepper, cheese or mushrooms, or any other filling you want to add like onions or tomato, and a little butter and oil. The first thing to do is break the eggs into a bowl and add salt and pepper. Add a little milk and then mix the eggs with a fork. In a frying pan, add half a teaspoon of butter and oil. Put it on the cooker and heat the butter and oil. When the butter melts and the oil is hot, pour in the eggs. When the eggs are cooking, add the cheese or mushrooms or another filling, and then fold the omelette in half and serve. Have a good meal!

13a The weather
Track 38
SOUND EFFECTS

Track 39
SOUND EFFECTS

Track 40
Natasha: Oh, look outside.
Khaled: Why? What's the weather like?
Natasha: It's raining and I don't have an umbrella.
Khaled: Don't worry – you can have my umbrella. I'm wearing my raincoat today.
Natasha: Oh, thank you – that's very kind.

Track 41
Look outside.
What's the weather like?
Don't worry.
That's very kind.

14a At the doctor's
Track 42
I've got a cold.
I've got a stomach ache.
I've got backache.
I've got a cough.
I feel sick.
My throat is sore.

Track 43
1
Receptionist: Good morning. How can I help you?
Sharif: Have you got any free appointments today?
Receptionist: Who is your doctor?
Sharif: My doctor's name is Hu. Dr Hu.
Receptionist: OK. There's an appointment for three o'clock. Is that OK?
Sharif: Do you have any for this morning? I've got a really bad stomach ache.
Receptionist: There's an appointment with Dr Livingstone at 11.30.
Sharif: OK, 11.30 with Dr Livingstone.

2
Dr Livingstone: Hello. Come in and sit down. I'm Dr Livingstone.
Sharif: Hello.
Dr Livingstone: How can I help you? What's the matter?
Sharif: I've got a stomach ache and my throat is sore.
Dr Livingstone: I see. Are you taking anything for this?
Sharif: No, doctor.
Dr Livingstone: OK, let me have a look at your throat. Uh-huh.
Sharif: Is it bad?
Dr Livingstone: No, not really. Take this prescription to the chemist. Come back to see me next week.
Sharif: Thank you very much.

15a Sending a parcel
Track 44
1
Customer A: Can I have a first-class stamp, please?
Assistant: Yes, here you are. Is that everything?
Customer A: Have you got an envelope?
Assistant: No, we don't sell envelopes.

2
Assistant: Hello. What can I do for you?
Customer B: Can you put £5.00 on my gas card, please?
Assistant: Could you put your card in the machine, please?
Customer B: OK.
Assistant: There you go, madam. £5.00 gas.

3
Assistant: Could you put the parcel on the scales, please?
Customer C: OK.
Assistant: And is that international or national?
Customer C: It's to London.
Assistant: So that's £2.46 first class.

Track 45
Can I have a first-class stamp, please?
Have you got an envelope?
Can you put £5.00 on my gas card, please?

16a After you
Track 46
1
Monika: Pardon me, is this the end of the queue?
Man 1: Yes, it is.

2
Khaled: Excuse me, would you like to sit here?
Man 2: Oh, thank you very much.
Khaled: Not at all. I'm getting off soon.

3
Isra: Excuse me, is this seat free?
Man 3: I'm sorry, someone's sitting there.
Isra: OK – thanks anyway. … Excuse me, is this seat free?
Woman: Yes, it is. Please take it.
Isra: Oh, thanks very much.
Woman: You're welcome.

4
Ahmed: After you.
Man 4: No, no – after you.
Ahmed: No, no – you first.
Man 4: No, please, you first …

Track 47
Pardon me.
Excuse me.
After you.
Is this the end of the queue?
Is this seat free?
Thanks anyway.
You're welcome.
Not at all.